AN AUTHOR
WHO HAS
SUFFERED FOR HIS ART

Peter Moore is an itinerant hobo who is lucky enough to be able to support his insatiable travel habit through writing.

In doing so he has become the voice of alternative travel both in Australia and the UK. He writes a regular travel feature for *TNT* magazine and has knocked out travel articles for the *Sydney Morning Herald*, the *Times* in London, the *Sun Herald* and the *Australian*. He is also a regular on the Triple J Morning show, and the website for *No Shitting in the Toilet* continues to pull in the hits and the awards.

In his travels, Peter has survived a shipwreck in the Maldives, a gas heater explosion in Istanbul, student riots in Addis Ababa and the continuing free fall of the Australian dollar. He survived a confrontation with the legendary Big Nambas tribe in Vanuatu and rates his first encounter with an Asian-style toilet as one of his life's defining moments. At last count he had visited 90 countries but, sadly, still has to doss on friends' sofas whenever he is in London.

When he is not lugging his senselessly overweight backpack through Third-World countries, Peter can be found at home in Sydney watching *Neighbours*. Sad really.

www.**booksattransworld**.co.uk

Praise for *No Shitting in the Toilet*

'Peter Moore is the Jim Carrey of Australian travel writing. I took a long time to review this book because I couldn't stop laughing'
ELISABETH KING, *SYDNEY MORNING HERALD*

'The cheeky, anecdote-packed book—a spin-off from an Internet site Moore created in 1995—was born when he became aware that traditional guide books failed to accurately describe "what it's like to be in these absurd situations and still end up loving it" '
WHO WEEKLY, 'INSIDE SCOOP'

'Peter Moore's travel guide may well be the most useful of its genre a traveller—novice or seasoned—could select...Whether you're actually going anywhere or just thinking about it, this book is a hoot'
STEPHANIE DALE, *QUEENSLAND TIMES*

Praise from the Internet

'THE funniest website I've encountered ... My [book] order is on its way!'
ANDY, UK

'Bought your book as a present for a friend and am currently pressing it under telephone books to get rid of the well-thumbed evidence of prior use. I only meant to glance at a few pages—honest!—and ended up reading pretty well the whole thing'
EIREAN JAMES, AUSTRALIA

Also by Peter Moore

THE WRONG WAY HOME
THE FULL MONTEZUMA

and published by Bantam Books

NO SHITTING

IN THE

TOILET

THE TRAVEL GUIDE
FOR WHEN YOU'VE
REALLY LOST IT

PETER MOORE

BANTAM BOOKS

LONDON · NEW YORK · TORONTO · SYDNEY · AUCKLAND

NO SHITTING IN THE TOILET
A BANTAM BOOK : 0 553 81451 6

First publication in Great Britain

PRINTING HISTORY
Bantam edition published 2002

3 5 7 9 10 8 6 4 2

Bantam Books are published by Transworld Publishers,
61–63 Uxbridge Road, London W5 5SA,
a division of The Random House Group Ltd,
in Australia by Random House Australia (Pty) Ltd,
20 Alfred Street, Milsons Point, Sydney, NSW 2061, Australia,
in New Zealand by Random House New Zealand Ltd,
18 Poland Road, Glenfield, Auckland 10, New Zealand
and in South Africa by Random House (Pty) Ltd,
Endulini, 5a Jubilee Road, Parktown 2193, South Africa.

Text design by Andrew Hoyne Design

Printed and bound in Great Britain by
Clays Ltd, St Ives plc.

ACKNOWLEDGEMENTS

Although they begged me not to (for reasons that will become more apparent the further you get into this book), I'd like to thank the following people for helping me get *No Shitting in the Toilet* off the ground.

My thanks go to Jacqueline Barrett, for putting up with my long absences; Shona Martyn, for taking a chance; Heather Curdie, for sorting out my problem with apostrophe's; Fiona Inglis, for handling all that agent stuff; and Garth Nix, for advice on getting published. Cheers as well to Richard MacDonald, Simon Taylor and Antony Harwood for helping *NSITT* finally see the light of day in the UK.

I should also thank all my travelling mates—especially Sean Henry, Tracy Simkins, Neil Smith, Stuart Martin, Donna Gunn, Peter Cruickshank and the Foster-Mitchell sisters—for the good times, the bad times and the times I can't quite remember. A big thank you as well to all the local people who have fed me, sheltered me and gone out of their way to help me on the road. Without them I would probably be living under a park bench somewhere.

Finally I'd like to thank Alby Mangels for making *World Safari I, II* and *III*. Even if the world isn't all sunken treasure and chamois bikinis, Alby instilled in me a sense of adventure and inspired me to get out and see the world. For that I am eternally grateful.

CONTENTS

INTRODUCTION

No Shitting in the Toilet is named after a sign I saw on the door of the toilet at Jack's Cafe in Dali, Yunnan Province, in China.

The sign was a crude, hand-painted representation of one of those internationally ubiquitous 'forbidding signs'—you know, the circle with a slash through it and a picture of the forbidden action or item in the middle. But instead of a camera or a dog or an icecream, this sign featured a little man squatting. Although you couldn't see the strain on his face, you could see the product of his labours. Just in case you didn't understand the sign, Jack had placed a grate over the top of the toilet as well.

The sign appealed to me because it pretty much sums up my philosophy of travel. It never quite turns out as you expect. You end up in situations that defy logical and rational thinking. Yet you end up having a brilliant time, not in spite of these situations, but because of them.

I guess that's also the philosophy behind this book—and the reason that **NSITT** isn't a *normal* travel guide.

Sure, it might look like a normal travel guide in its choice of topics and structure but, in fact, it's quite the opposite. Instead of practical hints, it gives you impractical ones. Rather than tell you the best places to stay, it tells you the worst. Instead of celebrating transcendental travel experiences, it revels in the most base and demeaning ones.

In that sense **NSITT** is more in touch with the way things really are. The world of **NSITT** is a world where you're more likely to find a cockroach on your pillow than a complimentary mint. It's a world where waiters would rather die than wish you a nice day, where you take your life into your own hands every time you get on a bus. It's a world where everything goes wrong and you still end up loving every minute of it.

Does the word perverse spring to mind? I hope so. Perversity is the essence of travel, and it's the essence of **NSITT**.

HOW TO USE THIS BOOK

No Shitting in the Toilet is based on a format used by more practical travel guides. It is divided into chapters based on topics of general interest to travellers. But with **NSITT** you get the added bonus of a totally irrelevant and impractical Top 10 tacked onto the end. The topics range from the more philosophical concerns of why and where through to the more practical topics of drinking and eating.

The format of **NSITT** is such that you don't have to start from the beginning and work your way sequentially through the book. In fact, it's probably better if you don't. Just pick a topic that interests you and dive right in. It will all begin to make sense after a while, although probably not until a couple of months after you finish the book and you try to use a piece of its scurrilous advice.

Similarly, if you're about to go travelling, you might want to start with a topic that is appropriate to your needs. When you're in the taxi out to the airport, perhaps you could read the chapter on where to go travelling. As you're kicking back in a dimly lit hospital in Indonesia, you might want to read the chapter on health and give the doctors a few tips on what may be ailing you.

If you're an armchair traveller, try using some of the advice found in **NSITT** in your daily life at home. Let's face it, bus drivers are the same the world over.

1

I guess finally I should cover the legalities, even if it is just to keep my publisher and lawyers happy. Basically, if the advice in this book doesn't land you in jail or get you into serious trouble, if it doesn't leave you stranded or ripped off, if it doesn't cause you to have the worst holiday you've ever had—well, you just haven't tried hard enough.

Happy shitting!

2

So you've decided to chuck it all in and go travelling. It would probably be the best decision you have ever made if it wasn't for all the stupid and inane questions everyone has started asking you. Let's start with the most annoying and most basic of all. It's 'Why?' and here's how you answer it.

So, why *are* you going travelling then?

Most people go travelling because they are running away from something. If you were to be honest with yourself, that's probably why you're going travelling too. Bad grades, bad relationship, nagging parents, armed robbery—they're all perfectly good reasons for grabbing a backpack and slipping out of the country.

I can't tell people that. They won't believe me!

That's true. Most people will expect a much deeper, more philosophical answer from you. Conditioned by centuries of pre-journey rationalisation, the simple truth is not enough for them. Just make something up that sounds politically correct, like a need to experience different cultures or a desire to see the destruction being wrought on our planet first hand. If struggling, find a Greenpeace brochure. They're often a handy source of inspiration.

If you are uncomfortable with that line of reasoning or you know that people simply just won't buy it, try the more enigmatic 'Because I need to'. Coupled with a slightly pained expression, it is enough to satisfy all but the most indiscreet of inquisitors.

How will I know when it is time for me to go travelling?

The signs are different for each person. We all have our own idiosyncrasies that come into play and signal that it is time to hit the road. There are some universal telltale signs, however, and they include the following:

o   You start to enjoy photocopying files.

o   You automatically get into the railway carriage that lines up exactly with the staircase on the platform of your destination.

o   A career in retail banking doesn't seem so bad after all.

o   Washing your car is the highlight of your weekend.

o   You've racked up three years' worth of annual leave and didn't even realise it.

o   You find yourself talking about your job at dinner parties, down the pub and to the bum who stops you for some small change.

I have a well paid, respected career. What excuses can I use for irresponsibly chucking it all in?

The wonderful thing about travel is how easily it can be justified to future employers. With a little thought and planning you can convince anyone thinking of hiring you that the three months you spent in the Bahamas smoking drugs and getting laid was an in-depth study tour of international banking systems. In fact, the more outrageous the story, the more likely an employer will swallow it.

I once met a couple of Americans from San Francisco who spoke of their journey through Asia as a means of familiarising themselves with future Pacific Rim trading partners. They argued that by exposing themselves to the different cultures and their trading techniques, they would be better placed in future APEC negotiations. It was a convincing spiel and I was tempted to use it myself. The trouble was, these guys believed what they were saying. Americans can be funny like that.

I need a holiday. Isn't that reason enough?

Travel is not about relaxing or taking a break. It's about throwing yourself in the deep end and hoping like crazy that you don't drown. The word 'travel' for example comes from the Latin word 'travail'—meaning spending ridiculous amounts of money to be miserable, homesick and frightened.

No, seriously. I just want to stay in a five-star hotel and be waited on hand and foot.

That's not travelling. That's just transplanting your current lifestyle—or a projected image of how you want your lifestyle to be—to another country. If that's all you want out of a trip, why not use the money you'd spend travelling to put in a jacuzzi out the back and hire an out-of-work actor to bring you drinks?

OK. I want to live dangerously. How's that for a reason?

Travel will certainly provide ample opportunity for you to do that. And the good news is that you don't have to travel to the world's trouble spots to do it. Every time you climb into a tuk-tuk in Bangkok, eat from a roadside stall in Egypt or wander the streets of a major American city, you are taking your life into your own hands.

I want to see the sights

Who amongst us hasn't looked at a glossy brochure and decided to go somewhere just because of the rather spectacular picture of a natural or man-made wonder? Trouble is, when you get there, the reality is somewhat different.

There's a good reason for that. Travel brochures deal with fantasies, whereas travel deals with reality. How many people do you think would go to the trouble of traipsing to Egypt to see the pyramids if they realised that there was an apartment block built right next to them? Or dream of a gondola ride in Venice if told that it costs the equivalent of a small house to just to sit in one and the national debt of Argentina to get one chorus of 'O Sole Mio' out of the boatman?

I want to meet the locals

An admirable notion, but in reality a little hard to achieve. When you're travelling, chances are that the locals you meet are all trying to sell you something or provide you with a service. Whether that's drugs, a bus ticket or a bribe to get you off a trumped-up charge, the person you're dealing with isn't really interested in discussing their innermost feelings or the political realities of their country. They only want your money.

6

It could be argued that, regardless of their motives, these people are still locals. That's true, but I'm sure that hanging out with the foreign equivalent of a used car salesman isn't what you had in mind when you said you wanted to meet the locals.

I want to find myself

Mmmm. If you're having problems discovering yourself in a place where you can actually read all the signs, what makes you think it's going to be any easier where they're all in a foreign language?

Seriously though, if you're keen to find out that in reality you're a short-tempered, egotistical racist who can't handle the pressure of finding a room for the night without wanting to hit somebody, then this is a perfect reason. Travelling gives you plenty of opportunity for discovering those kinds of personality disorders.

TOP 10 REASONS FOR TRAVELLING

A lot of people will tell you that the reason they are travelling is to broaden their mind and deepen their understanding of the cultures they are visiting. They are lying. Scratch below the surface and you'll find that their real reasons are a lot less altruistic—and a lot more like the 10 reasons listed below.

7

1. To lose weight

It's amazing what unappetising, unhygienically prepared food will do to even the most troublesome of waistlines. Add a dose of giardiasis or anaemic dysentery and the kilos literally drop off. The best spots for this revolutionary approach to weight loss are Asia, Africa and most university canteens.

2. To learn another language

There's no doubt that you pick up a foreign language more quickly in the country where it is spoken. Thrown in the deep end, you'll be astonished how quickly you'll pick up words for things like 'toilet' and 'take me there quickly'. A word of warning, though, about language tips given to you by friendly locals. What they assure you is an innocent phrase is invariably coarse and vulgar, and likely to get you punched in the mouth.

3. To avoid work

Perhaps the best reason of all. If you still have doubts, think of your current daily routine. Now think of lying on a beach, drinking beers and flirting with the locals. Need I say more?

4. To develop initiative

If your boss or professors say you lack initiative, go to a foreign country and have all your money stolen. Your embassy will shun you, you'll have to rummage through garbage bins just to eat and you'll fight over park benches with bums whose curses you won't even understand. It might be unpleasant at the time but you'll end up with rat cunning that would do Gordon Gecko proud.

5. To get dinner party tales

Ever sat in stony silence at a dinner party, too ashamed to speak because you have nothing interesting to say? Go travelling. Then you'll be able to delight and amaze guests with tales about the time you were thrown in jail on the Pakistani border or when you shat your pants coming back from a restaurant in Kigali.

6. To bore people with your travel slides/photos/ and/or videos

How many times have you sat through a boring slide show put on by your friends or family and wished the floor would open up and swallow you? Travelling gives you the chance to return the favour.

● ●
A handy hint: Try to keep your photos out of focus, poorly framed and of mundane, ordinary things. When you show them to friends or family, linger on each slide and regale viewers with long-winded stories that are only vaguely related to the photo and go nowhere in particular. Always end with an unnaturally long pause and something like 'Um, I forget what I was going to say'.
● ●

7. To avoid debt collectors

If you owe money, preferably to institutional creditors, why not shoot through overseas? You have a good time, they have a hard time tracking you down, and if the amount is relatively insignificant they may well give up altogether. Of course, to avoid embarrassment at the airport check-in counter, you should leave well before they have contacted Interpol. Also be aware that there's every chance your credit cards will be cancelled while you're away.

8.   To learn money management skills

Similar to the reason above but in this one you actually learn to manage money responsibly. Set yourself the task of visiting an expensive country like Japan or Sweden with as little money as possible. If you can survive living on 10 cents a day in Tokyo or Stockholm, managing your budget back home will be a breeze.

9.   To make friends or find a lover

It's true. Travel is a great way to meet people. The usual social mores and values are thrown out the window and people are generally more open, carefree and uninhibited. Of course, unless you take some precautions, you could end up rather friendly with the staff down at the local STD clinic as well.

10.   To learn about other people and cultures

Travel is the quickest way to learn that behind that indecipherable foreign language and quaint national costume is a person with the same shortcomings, foibles and prejudices as yourself. Scary thought, isn't it?

10

Chapter 2

WHEN?

Despite what your mother may have told you, it's never too soon to go travelling. Nor is it ever too late. The best time to go travelling is as soon as you can afford to. So break open that piggy bank, sell that old bomb you call a car or get a loan off your granny. Just get on the road now and remember—the age of discovery is never over when you are the discoverer.

When should I go travelling?

In the words of the world's most famous Burger King customer, it's now or never. Sure, the money could be better spent getting an education or a new stereo. You've probably got important exams coming up or your job's on the line as well. But believe me, these are mere trifles. As soon as the three Ms—marriage, mortgage and midgets—come along the only travelling you'll be doing is down to the 7-Eleven to pick up nappies. Go now—before it's too late!

No seriously. How will I know when it's the right time for me to travel?

A number of factors and events will mystically converge to confirm that you have chosen exactly the right moment to travel. They include:

o   The airfare for your flight goes up in price the day before you pay for it.

o   There's an important exam or a major report due the day after you plan to get back.

o   Your sister announces her plans to get married while you are away.

o   Your car's registration is due two weeks before you go and the cost of the repairs it needs to pass inspection eat quite considerably into your holiday funds.

o That girl or guy you've been trying to get onto for years suddenly becomes interested in you at your going away party.

o Your country breaks off diplomatic relations with the government of your destination.

OK. That answers when to go. How will I know when it's time for me to stay somewhere?

A friend of mine would never leave a place until he'd had a good time there. Another friend would not leave a destination until he had learnt something encouraging about the people and their culture. Both are currently stuck in Brisbane.

I would never suggest that you set yourself such stringent criteria on what is in essence such an arbitrary decision. If you're having a good time—stay. If you've met someone you fancy and who fancies you—stay. If you're too buggered to move—stay. If the police are closing in on you—go.

When should I come home?

The consensus seems to be that you should come home when your money runs out. I don't necessarily go along with this. For some people that would mean that their holiday is over barely after it has begun. And, as I have already pointed out, for the resourceful traveller, running out of money can be the start of a rewarding and challenging holiday.

Better, I think, to come home when you start getting abusive and hostile towards the symbols of everyday aggravation while travelling—the hawkers, the touts, the hotel owners and immigration officials. That is unless the life you're coming back to is worse than rotting in a Third World jail.

Wherever I go, people tell me I should have been there 20 years ago. Am I too late?

Unfortunately, this is an annoying and unavoidable side-effect of travelling on well-trodden backpacker routes. There is always someone propping up a bar somewhere, going on and on about how this place or that place was so much better 20, 15, 10 or even 5 years ago.

Take heart from the fact that this tactic is mostly used by ageing backpackers. Unable to party as hard as the 'young Turks', they instead try to win their respect by telling tales about days of yore when the accommodation was cheaper, the locals friendlier and the grass more plentiful.

13

But isn't that true?

Of course. Bali was once a quaint tropical paradise without an Aussie beer gut in sight. And Europe was quite an affordable destination where a cappuccino was within reach of everyone. But hey, you were probably in nappies at the time. There's not much you can do about it now, is there?

Should I travel when there is a war, civil disturbance or famine?

Listen to organisations like the US State Department and its various counterparts, and you wouldn't step outside your front door. Organised tour groups are the same. A small trifle like a civil war or a massacre and they're out of there faster than a rat up a drain pipe. For the adventurous and enterprising traveller, finding a room suddenly isn't a problem any more.

That sounds fine in theory, but what's the reality?

Don't get me wrong, we're not talking Cook's tours here. There are real dangers but there are also real benefits.

For example, I recently visited Dubrovnik in Croatia. Before the current conflict in the former Yugoslavia it was one of the great tourist centres, with the medieval 'old' city jammed to bursting point in summer with overweight Germans in bermuda shorts. Now, apart from the occasional UN convoy en route to Sarajevo, a traveller pretty much has Dubrovnik to himself. And unless the Serbs start shelling the place again, it's probably safer than some of the less salubrious parts of New York.

It was a similar story in Rwanda. Visiting the mountain gorillas used to be like joining a queue for the toilets at a football match. After a few skirmishes and a bit of insurgency, me and a couple of friends found we had thirty gorillas all to ourselves.

I should point out, however, that this was before the Rwandans started hacking into each other. Visiting trouble spots often involves impeccable timing, polite manners and a terrible lot of luck.

What about travelling when the weather is a little dodgy?

Hey, why not? Extreme climatic conditions can add excitement to the dullest of destinations. Just imagine the joy of sweltering in the Gobi desert during a heat wave, the adrenalin rush of huddling under a bed in Brunei during the cyclone season or the sense of accomplishment that comes with surviving at any time of the year in Bangladesh!

Are there any times I shouldn't go travelling?

Of course. If you are about to come into an inheritance that depends on being by the said loved one's death bed or you are about to sit a supplementary for the exam you just failed, it's probably a good idea to hang around just a little bit longer. Of course there are also other factors like the weather, the season and availability of flights to take into account. You might want to check out the following Top 10 worst times to travel for more detailed advice.

TOP 10 WORST TIMES TO TRAVEL

Personally, I'd spend my whole life travelling if I could. But even I have to admit there are times when I'm on the road that I wish I had stayed at home. Here are 10 of those times.

1. Winter

Many travellers sing the praises of travelling in winter. They claim that unlike the peak seasons, during winter you have everything to yourself. This is true. But what exactly do you have all to yourself? All the museums and art galleries are closed. Hotels and pensioni are shuttered. And depending how far north or south you are, the sun will probably set just after lunch—only of interest if you get a kick out of walking down lonely windswept streets freezing your butt off.

15

2. Spring

At first glance, spring seems the perfect time to travel. The weather is delightful, accommodation is plentiful and cheap and you'll have the great museums and art galleries all to yourself. The locals are less likely to see you as a walking money tree and may even sit down for a chat and a cup of tea. Trouble is, this is also the time that you have to be studying for exams, preparing vital reports or paying back long-standing debts.

3. Summer

Summer is commonly referred to as the peak season—meaning peak crowds, peak prices and peak temperature. You should note that it is also the time that the tempers of fellow travellers are at their peak too.

Sure, everything is open. But chances are that won't make much difference. Everywhere you go you'll be confronted by a sign even more infuriating than Closed—FULL.

4.   Autumn

Like spring, autumn would seem a great time to travel. The skies are blue, the air is crisp and the colour of the leaves on the trees is turning. If it's been a particularly good summer, however, you could find yourself out on a limb. All the hotel and bars will be closed while the owners are out enjoying their summer takings.

5.   The wet season

When it rains in the tropics it really rains. Roads become impassable, rivers burst their banks and strange grey fungi start growing in your shoes and between your toes.

If you're really unlucky, you could get stuck in a steamy, mildew-ridden backwater cut off from the rest of the world for months on end. You'll sharpen your backgammon skills, but that's about it.

6.   The dry season

You may be tempted into thinking that the dry season allows more mobility in the tropics. Well, you'd be wrong. The roads that became rivers during the wet season become cratered moon surfaces in the dry season. While you may have spent months stuck in a mildew-ridden town in the wet season, during the dry you'll get stuck in a pothole—and the only skills you'll sharpen are bus-pushing ones.

7.   The hajj

Every year hundreds of thousands of Muslims make the pilgrimage, or hajj, to Mecca. The rich ones catch the plane. The rest take whatever they can. If you're travelling in an Islamic country at the time, you'll need the patience of a saint too. It could take weeks before you can get a ride.

8.   Bayram

Another Islamic festival, this time celebrating Abraham's thwarted attempt to sacrifice Isaac. Celebrated mainly in Turkey, the banks are closed for a week and the streets run red with the blood of a million sheep unlucky enough to be chosen as old Isaac's stand-in. While you're cursing your luck at being caught without any money, spare a thought for the sheep that died for that leather coat you just bought.

9. School holidays

Everything's full, and everywhere you go there are packs of spotty adolescents wandering about, not quite sure what to do with all their new-found hormones. Instead they experiment with getting drunk, getting stoned and getting smart. Just remember that you were like that once and hide somewhere for a couple of weeks until they all go away again.

10. Public holidays

Think of public holidays at home. Nothing is open, the beaches are packed and the roads are gridlocked with cars full of people who wished they had stayed at home. It's the same the world over.

18

Chapter 3

WHERE?

Funny question, 'Where?' It impacts on everything you've got to do, like buying a plane ticket, how much money you need to take and whether you know anyone there who you can stay with for free. In fact, it's probably the most important question you're going to have to ask yourself.

Where *should* I go?

Like so much else with travel, deciding where to go travelling is such a personal thing. One person's perfect destination is another's living hell. As such, there's no right place to go and no wrong places either.

19

Having said that, there are some places that should be avoided at all costs. The name Brisbane springs immediately to mind.

What should I take into account when I'm deciding where to go?

Deciding on a travel destination involves a lot of common sense. If you're something of a party animal who likes to frequent girlie bars, then a visit to Iran is probably not a particularly good idea. Similarly, if you fancy yourself as a bit of a gourmet, Africa should not be high on your list. Other things you should take into account include:

o **Money:** More specifically, how much you can spare? If you're hoping to go travelling on your last dole cheque, Martinez is a little out of the question, isn't it?

o **Language:** Like it or not, if you can't speak the national tongue, you're going to have problems being understood. But take heart. Sometimes that can be a good thing.

- o **Medical disorders:** Note that in many countries the medical profession has not progressed much since the Middle Ages.

- o **Personality disorders:** Note that in many countries the psychiatry profession has not progressed much since the Middle Ages.

- o **Time:** Note that in many countries the transport system has not progressed much since the Middle Ages.

Where can I get away from it all?

Some people mistakenly equate 'getting away from it all' with palm-fringed beaches in exotic tropical locales. Nothing could be further from the truth! Sure, that little beach in Thailand or the Caribbean may look like something straight out of a postcard. But what the postcard doesn't show you is the teeming masses of hawkers ready to descend upon you the moment you lay down to catch a few rays. So unless your idea of getting away from it all is having pineapples or carved salad spoons shoved down your throat, it's much better to stay at home, draw the blinds and not answer the door for two weeks.

Where can I find culture?

This is a question we Australians have been asking ourselves for decades. While as a nation we are no closer to finding an answer, I can give you some tips on where to find culture as a traveller.

Firstly, don't equate culture with old buildings and art galleries. Sure, the architecture of Europe and the works of the Grand Masters are magnificent. It's just that in peak season, trying to catch a glimpse of the Mona Lisa is a little like packing into a rugby scrum.

Nor should you confuse culture with the quaint traditional dances put on by the local tourist authorities. More often than not, they've been updated to make them more palatable to Western tastes and are performed by dancers who are moonlighting from the local strip joint down the road.

Seriously though, the real moments of culture are found sharing a cup of *cay* with a Turkish villager or lunch with an African truck driver. Although, in the case of lunch with the truck driver in Africa, the cultural moment is more likely to be bacterial.

Where can I meet someone?

Don't fall into the trap that many unwary singles fall into and go to a resort. Sure, the Club Med brochure is full of smiling, tanned spunks. But once you shell out your hard-earned life savings and actually go to such a place, you'll find them full of honeymooning Germans and ageing Brits trying to rekindle their days of passion. If you're really unlucky, they'll try and rekindle it with you.

Similarly, many people go on tours that cater especially for 18 to 35 year olds. Guys figure that the bus is going to be chockers with girls who don't want the hassle of individual travel but still want a little bit of fun. Girls figure that the bus is going to be full of guys who figure that the bus is going to be chockers with girls who don't want the hassle of individual travel but still want a little fun. The reality is one of the world's great enduring mysteries. Whether you are male or female, there will always be twice as many of your sex on the tour and they'll all be fighting over the driver or the cook, no matter how ugly they are.

Where can I find all the home comforts?

It's called home, and if that's all you're looking for you can save a lot of money by simply spending your holidays there.

Should I tailor my holiday plans around a special interest?

Perhaps. But just remember that travelling to India to do a bit of trainspotting, no matter how exotic or rare the rolling stock, does not make it any more socially acceptable than standing on a platform in an anorak doing the same thing at home. You will still be regarded by fellow travellers, and society as a whole, as a rather sad individual. Travel is about breaking routines, changing habits and sampling a whole new lifestyle. That is unless your lifestyle already consists of staying out late, getting drunk and having a good time.

Should having contacts in a particular place impact on where I go?

Of course! Having someone to stay with in a place like London or Tokyo means that you can afford to stay there for a matter of days instead of a matter of hours. In fact, some people plan their entire itinerary around the addresses of friends, acquaintances and people whose name they have picked at random from the phone book. Of course, for some people that means they never get out of their home town.

I still don't know where to go. What should I do?

Read some books. Watch some TV. Ask your friends about places they have been to. And if you still can't decide where to go, do one of two things. Firstly, give up all together on the idea of travelling and invest the amount you would have spent on a small futures portfolio. Or secondly, do what I do in similar situations: get a world globe, spin it vigorously, poke it with your index finger and go to wherever it lands. Thanks to this tried and true method I have visited such exciting places as Blackpool, Oodnadatta and an industrial estate just on the outskirts of Hoboken.

If that prospect doesn't excite you—though I can't understand why it wouldn't—you might want to browse through the brief guide of destinations I've provided below for inspiration.

The NSITT continent-by-continent guide

Africa

Sweeping savannah. Charging wildebeest. Fearsome Masai warriors. When it comes to Africa most travellers lose it and let their imaginations go wild. Unfortunately, that's about the wildest thing there is in Africa. The beasties are all in game parks and viewed from sanitised white vans. And the most dangerous predators you'll come across are tour operators and the girls at the Florida 2000 Bar in Nairobi.

Asia

If your idea of Asia is untouched cultures and lifestyles you'd better hurry up. The economic miracle that is most of Asia means that things are changing at an uncharacteristically, un-oriental pace. In the face of double-digit growth, it won't be long before even Buddhist monks trade in their orange robes for Italian business suits, and convert their ancient temples into McDonald's.

Europe

The cradle of Western civilisation is also the cradle of modern tourism. The Europeans have got the homogenising and packaging of culture down to a fine art. Don't get me wrong—the art, the architecture, the cafes and the culture are all still there. It just costs an arm and a leg to get your five minutes' worth. But then I'm an Australian and our dollar's about as useful as an Albanian lek. Europe's probably a stimulating, affordable experience for everyone else.

The Americas

This continent can be divided into three parts—the north, the middle and the south.

North America is worth visiting to check up on what you'll be watching on TV in a couple of years time and whether you should still be wearing your baseball cap backwards.

23

Central America is a great place to visit if you get off on civil disorder, natural disasters and a higher-than-average chance of getting shot.

South America is a mixture of both, with the added benefit of giving an insight into what the North American economies will be like in a decade or two.

Australia

The world's largest island and smallest continent, Australia is an amazing land of geographical contrasts, unique fauna and friendly locals. There's also quite a party scene on the backpacker trail so most travellers are too pissed to notice any of it anyway.

The Indian Subcontinent

Swamis, gurus, sadhus, lamas. It seems every second person in India has a spiritual bandwagon to push. And it seems every second traveller is keen to jump on board in search of the road to enlightenment. Some even find it—though usually on the fifteenth visit to the can after a particularly dodgy vindaloo.

TOP 10
FAVOURITE
DESTINATIONS

Favourite travel destinations are such a personal thing. A place that you thought was heaven on earth was probably a living hell for someone else. That's because it's the people you meet or the things that happen that make a place special. Having said that, I've listed my favourite 10, anyway. And if I do say so myself, you'd have to be hard to please if you didn't find something to like about these places.

1.   Istanbul, Turkey

Ahhh, old Constantinople. A mosque on every hill and a carpet salesman on every corner. Perched above the Bosphorus, it's a bustling, hustling amalgamation where Europe meets Asia. At sunset, grab yourself a kebab, sit on the seats outside the Blue Mosque and marvel at the beauty of the call to prayer floating from the minarets of a hundred different mosques. At 4 o'clock the next morning, curse the very same calls for disturbing your sleep.

24

2.   Budapest, Hungary

A lot of people plump for Prague in the battle of the Eastern European capitals, but I find the Czech capital a mite too prissy. That's something you can't accuse Budapest of. Grubby, derelict and scarred by the worst of Stalinist architecture, it still has a certain raw, experimental energy that's lacking in Prague. The girls dress like hookers, the guys dress like poets and they all hang out in clubs where you're just as likely to hear a thrash metal band as poetry readings.

3.   Luang Prabang, Laos

Sleepy isn't quite the word for this riverside town in central Laos. This former capital of a united Laos is positively comatose. Still, with its royal palaces, temples and caves, Luang Prabang *is* the historic, religious, social, artistic and cultural capital of Laos. The fact that you can still see the occasional HG Holden driving around is a good indication of how the world has largely passed this place by.

25

4.   The road to Jalalabad, Afghanistan

You've got to love a country where you can dress up and pose for photos with the local mujaheddin leader holding a loaded M16. Sure, the jihadic fighters wandering the streets with AK47s and the occasional grenade launcher are a bit of a worry but most seem to be too wired to even notice you're there. Definitely one to tell the grandkids about—if you survive.

5.   Eṣfahān, Iran

A lot of travellers rave about the Islamic architecture in this town, but for mine it's the tea shop under the Sī o Sé Pol bridge that makes a visit to Eṣfahān worthwhile. Built in 1602, it has 33 arches under which waiters dish out sweet tea and hookah pipes to local riffraff and luminaries. The tiny rooms in the base of each arch are connected by rickety planks only inches above the rushing river. While it may not be too much fun watching the waiters—they're much too skilful to ever fall in—visiting foreigners provide a wealth of entertainment possibilities.

6.   Lamu, Kenya

Lamu, an ancient Arab trading post off the coast of Kenya, is a bizarre mix of Arab and African cultures. The women still wear the modest Arab *chādor*, but when they start running about whistling and shrilling, it's pure African sexuality. And then there's the donkeys. If you're ever trapped behind one in any of the narrow lanes don't expect it to get out of your way. They own this town.

7.   Tierradentro, Colombia

It's not the ancient painted burial caves that make this place one of my favourite places in South America. Nor is it the spectacular setting amongst the huge rolling hills. It's the annual fiesta at the local whitewashed church. If you're lucky, the local drunk will start waving a knife about and shout 'Don't worry, I'm a butcher' at you in slurred Spanish.

8.   Siberut, Indonesia

Forget your expensive male bonding weekends, this is the real thing. The Mentawai people of Siberut, an island just off Padang in Sumatra, still get around in loincloths. And if you give them enough tobacco, they'll let you do it too. Don't expect to catch any monkeys with the bow and arrow they provide you with though. That's just for *their* amusement. When the Mentawai want to catch a monkey for dinner, they use a gun.

9.   Kathmandu, Nepal

A magical, mystical town that still holds its appeal despite the hordes of travellers in designer hiking gear. Sure Thamel is nothing more than an overgrown clothes shop but it's still fun to watch travellers step out in their new 'funky' threads, convinced that they actually look cool.

● ●

A sad note: Willy Bob, the legendary guru of Kathmandu who lifted blocks of stone with his bare penis, has passed away. His disciples have tried to carry on the tradition, but sadly, they're not up to it.

● ●

26

10.   Ko Pha-Ngan, Thailand

Ever since the cops got greedy at Goa, this has become the 'techno' capital of Asia. Every full moon the beach at Hat Rin is packed with foreigners showing off their best 'Big Box, Little Box' dancing techniques. Despite the ready availability of speed punch and magic mushroom pancakes, I suggest you try to stay straight. You could be rewarded, as I was, with the sight of a girl walking up to a Thai policeman saying 'Meow, I am a cat', complete with appropriate hand movements.

MONEY

In the words of that immortal ABBA song: 'Money, Money, Money. It's a rich man's world'. Or is it? Like many other things, it's not the size of your wallet that counts, it's how you use it. Anyway, here's the lowdown on lucre. And believe me, with the condition of the notes in some countries, it *will* be filthy.

How much money should I take?

The conventional wisdom is that you can never have too much money when travelling. While this seems quite sensible reasoning, I beg to differ. Rather, I would argue that what you get out of your trip increases exponentially the less money you have to spare.

It also depends on where you plan to go. In some countries you could sell your house to finance a two-week trip and still feel like a pauper. Yet in places like Africa and parts of the Middle East, you could live like royalty on the coins in that jar sitting on your desk.

The NSITT exchange rate primer

Many people view the world of international finance as a complex and mystifying world. In my travels, however, I have found that it operates on the following simple principles:

o   The money changer offering the best rates for traveller's cheques insists on seeing the proof of purchase receipt that you left in your hotel—or worse, at home.

o   The small transaction you want to make because you are leaving the next day incurs a 50 per cent commission.

27

- When you enter a new country with a pocketful of coins from the previous country, banks will refuse to exchange them, even though they add up to an amount equal to that country's foreign debt.

- Shopkeepers will refuse to take a tattered, torn, smelly note off you, even though they were the ones who gave it to you as change earlier in the day.

- The exchange rate you refuse on one side of the border is always better than the one you finally accept on the other side.

- You will always be caught short of cash in towns where there are no banks, no black market and no hotels or restaurants willing to take credit.

- Your country's currency is drastically devalued just before you leave.

- It miraculously re-values the moment you return home with a wad of foreign currency to exchange.

How should I carry my money?

Cash, traveller's cheques, plastic or a combination of all three. It's not an easy decision to make. But here are some hints to make it easier.

The benefits of taking cash

There's a lot to be said for travelling with a fistful of legal tender. Shopkeepers will mysteriously drop their prices for it. Taxi drivers will take you out of your way for it. Border officials will come over all helpful for it. However, there is one vital proviso—the currency you're carrying has to be either yen, marks or US dollars. Try pawing off Aussie dollars or Sri Lankan rupiah to the taxi driver in Saigon and he'll tell you to get out and walk.

Even if you happen to have one of the more desired currencies, there is also the security issue to take into account. No matter how good your insurance is, nobody is going to come to your aid if you have all your cash knocked off.

The benefits of traveller's cheques

Unlike cash, traveller's cheques do offer the advantage of being replaced if stolen. In fact, if you were to believe the American Express ads, a

28

little man will brave flesh-eating piranhas and malarial mosquitoes to bring your replacement cheques right to your door. Anyone who has ever had traveller's cheques stolen knows that it is never that easy. Staff at American Express offices the world over hold backpackers in slight regard. They will suspect, quite rightly in many cases, that you have sold your cheques to an international money-laundering concern.

Then there's the problem of cashing traveller's cheques in places where banking is barely beyond the Stone Age. Like Zaire, for instance. The tellers there won't cough up the cash unless your cheque has 'sample' stamped across the middle of it—just like the one in the book Amex sent them in 1965.

And then there is plastic

Now that even yurts in the backblocks of Mongolia have ATMs, you may be tempted to take along a credit card with you and just drag out money as the need arises. You should be cautious about doing this for a number of reasons.

Firstly, these ATMs dispense money in the local currency. Now while the Polish zloty may not be all that strong at the moment you pull out the cash, you can be rest assured that it will have strengthened unnaturally by the time your chosen credit company or bank finally gets around to processing your transaction.

The second reason is a horrible consequence of this. Your calculations on the balance of your credit limit will be terribly out of whack. It is a much studied, though little understood phenomenon that when you desperately need cash, you will have well and truly passed your credit limit. Not only that, the bailiffs will be haunting the airport on your return.

Goods to barter with

It used to be the case that you could take your old pair of Levis travelling with you, flog them to an appreciative local and live off the proceeds for a couple of months. Those days are long past. In Asia, the locals have moved onto less portable status symbols like BMWs and Italian designer furniture. In Russia, the other big market for the icons of Western decadence, they can barely afford to buy food, let alone a pair of jeans.

Should I deal on the black market?

The black market is a rather wondrous institution that exists in countries where the currency is being artificially propped up. If played correctly, it allows the traveller to get twice as much, sometimes a lot more, for his money. Played incorrectly, however, and the same traveller could end up broke, bruised or in jail.

How do I find the black market?

In most places where there is an active black market, this is something you won't have to worry about. Just walk down the street in all your Westerness and it will find you. In fact, in places like Kathmandu, you'll be convinced that your name has been changed to 'Change Money?'.

That's not to say you won't ever have problems. A friend of mine was stuck in the forgettable Tanzanian town of Mwanza without any Tanzanian shillings and spent the good part of two days searching out a man the locals called 'The Doctor' to change money with. He eventually found 'The Doctor' propping up the bar in the Victoria Hotel, with a stethoscope draped around his neck. Unfortunately the good doctor was too drunk to deal.

At a pinch, though, gold shops are usually a good place to look.

What tricks should I look out for?

Money certainly brings out inventiveness in people. I am constantly in awe of the magical schemes and tactics used by people to try to part me and my money whenever I try to change a bit on the side. Some of the better known tricks developed by black marketeers to rip you off include:

o Counting out notes and then, by sleight of hand, giving you less.

o Folding notes in half so it appears you get more than you do.

o Getting an attractive member of the opposite sex to flirt with you and distract you.

o Interspersing the real notes with notes no longer in circulation.

o Interspersing the real notes with similar looking notes from another country that are worth even less.

o And the old favourite, pulling out a knife.

Should I lend money to other travellers?

This is the surest way to lose money. While there is always the possibility that you might come out of a black market deal slightly ahead, you have absolutely no chance of seeing your money again if you lend it to a fellow traveller. A friend of mine is still waiting for the US$100 he lent a Canadian girl seven years ago.

Having said that, there is sometimes an unexpected bonus to lending a struggling traveller a helping hand. They may be a billionaire who, touched by your generosity, will nominate you as sole beneficiary in their will. Or, more likely, your act of kindness may be rewarded with another. I once paid for a room for a French couple in Bali because, not surprisingly, the owner of this particularly flea-bitten establishment didn't have change for a US$100 note. Not only did this couple track me down and pay me back the money, they also shouted me an amazing breakfast at one of Bali's better hotels. It's like everything with travel. You've just got to trust your instincts.

Should I bargain for things?

Of course! Bargaining, haggling, or whatever you want to call it, is one of the most invigorating, enjoyable and challenging aspects of being a backpacker. While it can be a little daunting at first, once you get something for a tenth of the asking price there'll be no holding you back.

Souvenirs, accommodation, transport, food—once you put your mind to it, there's nothing you can't haggle for. In fact, a friend and I once haggled a traffic fine in Bali down to half the initial asking price! Just work from the principle that everyone is scandalously ripping you off and you'll be fine.

31

One unfortunate aspect of travelling is that travellers often come home entrenched with the notion of questioning every price. You'll often see these sad individuals at the railway station back in their home town arguing with a ticket vending machine even as the men in white coats drag them away.

How will I know when I have got a good price?

Most guidebooks suggest that if the hawker or shop owner smiles at your price you are pretty close to the mark. I find that haggling with them until they chase you out of the shop is a more accurate indication.

Where is the safest place to keep my money?

Basically anywhere except in the safe at your hotel, pensione or losmen. These only serve to make life easy for the biggest crooks around—the owners of the said hotel, pensione, or losmen. They don't have the hassle of searching around your room or in your bags while you sleep. And they have a cosy 'relationship' with the local constabulary so that when you report the theft to them no one can speak English any more.

Money belts are also a no-no. Any mugger worth his salt knows that if he robs a backpacker he'll find enough cash strapped around the backpacker's gut to start a small Third World business venture.

The bottom line is this. You don't take all your life savings with you at home, so don't do it while you are travelling. Split it up and hide it in different spots. And if you end up forgetting where you've put half of it, don't worry. It will make for a pleasant surprise on your next trip. Though how useful a couple of thousand Turkish lire will prove in Guangdong Province, China, is anybody's guess.

32

What do I do if I am robbed?

Cable home to mum and dad to send you more money. It will be a lot quicker than relying on the police or the traveller's cheque company to sort something out. Don't even bother with your embassy. They'll just send you home on the most expensive flight available and then gleefully extract the fare from your income tax for the next couple of decades.

TOP 10 RIP-OFFS

Getting ripped off is a natural and beneficial consequence of travelling. It happens, and in many ways it's the best preparation you can get for the many rip-offs that lie ahead in your life—like your first mortgage for example.

Anyway, here are 10 of the more inventive scams I've come across over the years.

1. The bank on the Uganda/Zaire border

Not so much a bank as a thatched hut to the side of the border post. The immigration officer in charge will take you there to change money at a quarter of the going rate before stamping you into Zaire. There is some semblance of officialdom though—an exchange rate form that was typed out circa 1963.

2. The boat ride from Sintang to Putussibau, West Kalimantan

No one in their right mind would pay close to US$100 for a speed boat ride up the Kapuas river from Sintang to Putussibau. Yet there's a gaggle of Indonesian boat owners hanging about Sintang wharf in aviator sunglasses convinced that you will. And you know what, there's a steady stream of Westerners willing to do just that. Sintang can do that to a person.

3. A slice of pizza, Venice

Is a slice of pizza worth the same as a small family sedan? The pizzeria owners of Venice seem to think so. And, judging by the amount of custom they get each summer, the average tourist does too.

4. Changing money with the Turkish train guard, Athens to Istanbul 'Express'

It seems after the 36-hour train ride from Athens, bleary-eyed travellers will agree to anything—including exchanging money with Turkish guards as this ancient train winds its way along the Bosphorus into Istanbul. A friend of mine lost 30 per cent on the standard rate and a packet of Marlboro which the guard nicked while he slept.

5. Duty free shopping in Hong Kong

It may be the duty free capital of the world, but a lot of travellers get a lot less than they bargained for. The box may well bear all the markings of the item you bought but what is actually inside is anybody's guess. It could be a lesser model or if you're really unlucky, a brick.

6. Any meal in Africa

34

I defy anyone to gaze upon a plate of ugali and claim that they haven't been ripped off. Even if they got it for free.

7. Train fares in London

Mile for mile, the London Underground is more expensive than flying on the Concorde. Worse still, you don't get the free booze, a meal served on proper china or the comfy seat either. I don't think they have anyone standing in the aisles on the Concorde either.

8. Gems bought in Bangkok

On arriving in the capital of old Siam, you will probably be approached by someone claiming that it is a special holiday for Buddhist monks. He will also tell you that you are very lucky because a certain gem shop he knows of is celebrating the occasion by offering very special deals on precious gems. Don't be fooled by the official Thai government certificates of authenticity. The Thais are doing amazing things with cubic zirconia these days.

9. Transport and accommodation in China

Can you think of any sane reason why a foreigner should pay two or three times more for everything than a local Chinese person? Nor can I. Yet that's what happens every day in China on everything from train and bus fares through to accommodation. I guess while people are silly enough to pay it, the Chinese government will continue this insidious form of racial discrimination. I'll just step down from my soapbox, shall I?

10. Victoria Falls—the Zimbabwe side

Not the falls themselves—they're well worth any price of admission—rather the fact that it costs US$20 to see them from Zimbabwe, yet only US$3 on the Zambian side. Same falls, same drenching spray, even the same African art hawkers. Why give President Mugabe the extra 17 bucks when you can buy a life-size soapstone hippopotamus with the money instead?

35

36

Chapter 5

GUIDEBOOKS

What tells lies, indulges in scandalous exaggeration, constantly gets things wrong, is chronically unreliable, massively overweight and costs a small fortune to maintain?

No, it's not your new lover, it's a travel guidebook. And this is your guide to whipping it into shape.

Can guidebooks be trusted?

Tricky question that. Guidebooks are a little like politicians. They start off with the best intentions, but often get waylaid by reality along the way.

It's best to treat guidebooks as you would an absent-minded and unreliable friend. They'll put you in the vague vicinity of a cheap hotel or restaurant, but just don't expect them to take you to the exact spot. Thankfully they are a little better with railway stations and bus terminals. They tend to be where they have always been.

A lot of it has to do with the fact that it can take up to 10 years for a guidebook to be researched, written and published. Also, guidebook writers can't be everywhere and have to rely on other travellers for information. I once met a guidebook writer at Bong's Guest House in Tanjung Pinang in Indonesia. I was heading south to Dabo and he asked if I could send him information for an Indonesian travel kit he was compiling. If I'm any indication of the riffraff guidebook writers rely on for research, no wonder they end up getting some things horribly wrong.

37

When should I be cautious about suggestions made by a guide-book?

Many travellers believe that anything suggested by a guidebook should be treated with the utmost caution. But these are generally the kind of travellers that sleep in public conveniences and boast about travelling on 53 cents a day. If you work on the principle that the prices will be three times more than quoted, half the hotels will have fallen down and most of the restaurants closed by the health authorities, you should be okay.

There are some suggestions, however, that should be dismissed out of hand. They include:

o Any floating or revolving restaurant described as serving good food at reasonable prices.

o An international standard hotel described as being surprisingly good value.

o Any railway journey that is described as having unmissable scenery. The service will either be long abandoned or only running at night.

o Any market described as being used only by locals. What they really mean to say is that the market is used exclusively by locals to rip tourists off.

Should I read my guidebook before I go?

Good God no! Have you ever travelled with someone who has read up on a city before they get there? They spend the whole trip intent on visiting all the wonderful things that they have read about in their guidebook. Despite the fact that many of these sights—natural, man-made or otherwise—are a major disappointment, they will continue to traipse around a foreign city until every suggestion has been seen, sampled and photographed.

38

It is better, I think, to read the appropriate guidebook just as you are leaving a city. Then you can pass the journey regretting all the things you missed and torturing yourself with their imagined wonder. Having travelled extensively, I can tell you that they are much better in your imagination.

Should I take a guidebook with me?

Hey, why not? Even if you don't consult it very often, it can serve a host of other purposes. You could entertain other travellers by reading out your favourite blatantly incorrect passages. You could offer it to another traveller you've had your eye on as a means of breaking the ice. Or if you get really desperate, you could use it to start a small fire, line your clothes for insulation or as food should you ever get hungry.

Do guidebooks have personalities?

My word! There are a million and one guidebooks out there and each one of them has their very own strengths, shortcomings and idiosyncrasies. In fact, choosing a guidebook to accompany you on your travels is as personal a decision as buying a new pair of shoes or a new coat. If you're not comfortable with it, you're going to have a terrible time.

The NSITT guide to guidebooks

To help you decide on which guidebook is right for you, I've put together a little primer on a few of the 'major' players. Please remember that these are just my personal opinions. Before making your final decision I suggest you take your prospective guidebook home to meet your parents or, at the very least, let it see you when you are drunk or without make-up.

Let's Go

Updated annually by roving packs of American college students, the Let's Go guides accurately reflect the wants and needs of the average travelling college student—clean accommodation, bland food and the names of nightclubs and bars that don't frown upon fraternity antics.

Ideal for those wanting to meet other college students and who are determined to see the maximum amount of countries possible on their Eurail pass.

Moon Publications

As the title suggests, drippy, hippy guides that haven't woken up to the fact that the sixties are over. The Grateful Dead of travel guides, they believe that travelling is a spiritual experience and seem determined to help you make it an out-of-body one.

Still, the notes on local culture, traditions and customs are extensive and useful for memorising to impress folk who just wouldn't understand that you spent your entire trip to Indonesia under the influence of alcohol.

Rough Guides

Aimed at the more discerning backpacker, the Rough Guides mix the budgetary constraints of your average traveller with the cultural ideals of the more cultured types. They get a bit too detailed for mine, but then that's just the British trainspotter heritage coming through.

Frommer's

The guide for those who feel too old to backpack but not rich enough to travel in style. One step above the hostel route, the Frommer's guides first made their name telling holidaying accountants how to travel in Europe for $5 a day. Interesting to note that the figure has now shot up to $100 a day and the hostels are back in vogue.

Fodor's

I've never looked at one so I don't know. Don't know if I'll ever have enough money to ever consider using one anyway.

Lonely Planet

My guidebooks of choice, and not just because they're the only internationally successful thing to come out of Australia. The Lonely Planet guides seem to have the happy knack of striking a balance between making a place sound interesting without hiding its warts. And if a place is a shithole, they'll generally tell you so. I also kind of like their laconic Aussie outlook.

That's not to say LP don't get it wrong. Possibly because I do use them most frequently, if you check out my top 10 bum steers at the end of this chapter you'll notice that Lonely Planet provide the majority of them. And they have had a tendency of late to employ earnest American writers. Hopefully it is just a temporary aberration.

Why are there so many rumours about guidebook authors?

It is a bizarre consequence of the phenomenal increase in backpacking worldwide that a 'cult of personality' has sprung up around many of the better-known authors. Some sad individuals even get a kick out of gathering in bars and exchanging these rumours.

Tony Wheeler, the founder of Lonely Planet, for example, is supposed to have died in a motorcycle accident in India, been eaten by a lion in Africa and hit by a tram in Melbourne. Geoff Crowther, the legendary author of *Africa on a Shoestring*, supposedly never touches anything stronger than water. And Bill Dalton, who wrote the *Indonesian Handbook*, is rumoured to be a radical celibate.

> The only rumour that I have been able to substantiate, simply by comparing the author's photographs, is that Tom Brosnahan, the creator of Lonely Planet's guide to Turkey, had more hair when he wrote the third edition than he did when he wrote the first. Why, of course, is still a mystery. The most plausible explanation I have heard is the curative effects of the hot springs at Pamukkale.

41

Are guidebooks purpose driven?

No doubt most guidebooks set out to be a universal one-size-fits-all guide to their chosen demographic. But more often than not they end up developing an expertise all of their own.

Take the *Indonesian Handbook* put out by Moon Publications for example. Written by Bill Dalton, it turns out to be one of the most detailed accounts of the whorehouses of Indonesia you'd ever want to come across. Sure, there's a lot of stuff about the more conventional Indonesian local customs and traditions. But when Bill gets on to the special lovemaking techniques of the Madurese women, I get the impression he's on a subject he's particularly passionate about.

Similarly, Tom Brosnahan turns the Lonely Planet's guide to Turkey into a primer on high school physics. He suggests that travellers take all the containers holding liquids onto the bus with them, so that they can gently ease open the caps as the pressure drops on the more mountainous stretches of road in Turkey. The only time I found this useful was on particularly terrifying stretch of road and when the container was glass and holding hard liquor.

Can a guidebook be overly cultural?

Most definitely. Should you buy one of those tomes, like the rarefied Blue Guides for example, you'll end up spending your whole trip searching for the resting place of an obscure emperor or some filigree in a forgotten corner of a forgotten temple. On finding the place, you may well discover that the said emperor's headstone has been stolen, broken, or most likely, not worth the effort.

What if I get a sneaking suspicion that the guidebook may be wrong?

Go with your instincts. You're most likely to be right when a guidebook says that a major hotel is surprisingly good value or that a floating or revolving restaurant represents an extraordinarily affordable dining experience. As any traveller knows, such things are physically impossible. If they did exist, it would have only been temporary, lasting barely beyond the writer's visit and the men in white coats coming to take the manager away.

42

Should I treat my guidebook as a bible?

Why not? Most guidebooks are like the Old Testament—full of fanciful inaccuracies that describe a mystical time in the past when everything was brighter, cheaper and more plentiful. The only difference is that not much 'begetting' goes on in guidebooks. Unless you've got the second edition of Bill Dalton's *Indonesian Handbook*, that is.

You will notice in your travels a lot of the locals will exhort you not to treat your guidebook as a bible. They will cajole you into ignoring the price listed or the missing bathrooms. They encourage you to use the book only as a rough indication and argue that things change and prices go up. They are usually the owners of a hotel mentioned in a guidebook who, now that business is booming, figure they can charge pretty much what they want.

Should I avoid places suggested by guidebooks then?

Regardless of how enticing a place sounds in a guidebook, you should try avoiding any place a guidebook specifically recommends or raves about. That is, of course, unless you get off on seeing people walking around clutching the self-same guidebook dodging huge tourist buses loaded with camera-totting Germans.

Don't be fooled when a guidebook describes a place as being 'little-visited' either. You could end up arriving somewhere only to find it isn't little-visited anymore. Or worse still, you'll discover the reason why it wasn't visited very often in the first place.

If guidebooks aren't reliable, what advice is?

Quite simply, the advice you'll get from fellow travellers. They have been there and done that and probably within the past couple of days. And if you meet them in the guesthouse you're staying in or the restaurant you're eating at, chances are they are on a similar budget to you.

Failing that, try the visitor's book at any Australian embassy. Unlike most other embassies, Australian embassies are used almost exclusively by backpackers, so the visitor's books are often full of helpful advice on accommodation, transport and political conditions. Using the visitor's book at the Australian Embassy in Nairobi, I was able to find the only guesthouse in Nairobi offering continuous hot water.

TOP 10 BUM STEERS

Discovering inaccuracies is part of the bonding process between you and your chosen guidebook. It shows that, like you, they are prone to mistakes. Having said that, here are 10 examples when the friendship with my guidebooks was severely tested.

1. The Floating Restaurant, Hue

> *Vietnam: a travel survival kit*
> Lonely Planet Publications, 2nd edition, 1993

It had always been my experience with floating restaurants that they serve crappy food, hire surly waiters, charge like wounded bulls and are invariably situated over the town's main sewerage outlet. So I was going against all my instincts when I recently visited the Floating Restaurant in Hue on the recommendation of my Lonely Planet guidebook.

It described the restaurant as being 'justifiably known for good service, outstanding Vietnamese cuisine [not food, cuisine!] and low prices'. It might just have been the night I visited, but I found the food crappy, the waiters surly, the prices stratospheric and the location a little on the whiffy side.

2. Erzurum Oteli, Trabzon

> *Turkey: a travel survival kit*
> Lonely Planet Publications, 3rd edition, 1990

I should point out here that Tom Brosnahan is one of my all-time favourite guidebook writers, and that I rather enjoy his little dissertations, simplistic though they are, on high school physics and the importance of using a handbrake on a

44

steep incline. It's not his fault that the Erzurum Oteli—which he charmingly describes as a haven of old men playing backgammon under sweet-scented honeysuckle—has closed down. Nor is he responsible for the fact that a less scrupulous and less savoury establishment across the road has changed its name to lure in unsuspecting travellers looking for a quick game of dominos and views of the sea.

3. The Ashok Yatri Niwas hotel, Delhi

India: a travel survival kit
Lonely Planet Publications, 2nd edition, 1984

The Ashok Yatri Niwas is described as 'a new hotel with such excellent facilities at such a low cost that it's really difficult to believe it's there'. Follow the corresponding map and it's not. Through the slip of the mapmaker's pen, the Yatri Niwas is a good couple of kilometres further out of town than it really is.

45

I spent an entire afternoon wandering up and down Panchkuin Marg, swatting off persistent auto-rickshaw drivers and ignoring their exhortations that I was going the wrong way and that the Yatri Niwas was too expensive for me anyway. When I finally found it, I discovered that they were right on both counts. It's a pretty sad state of affairs when you can believe a rickshaw wallah ahead of your guidebook!

4. The five-legged cow in Yogya Zoo, Yogyakarta

Indonesia Handbook
Moon Publications, 2nd edition, 1983

It was my first trip abroad and I was young and impressionable. I read in my guidebook, the legendary 2nd edition of the *Indonesia Handbook* by Bill Dalton, that there was a five-legged cow in Yogya Zoo. So I spent an entire afternoon frightening zoo staff by saying 'lima' (Indonesian for five), slapping my leg and mooing.

I could still very well be there, if not for one particularly terrified gardener calling the police. One of the officers could speak English and told me that the cow had died years ago. It was my first experience of the power of guidebooks to completely and utterly 'possess' travellers, and very nearly put me off them for life.

5.   The mute cafe owner, Lac Thahn Restaurant, Hue

Vietnam: a travel survival kit
Lonely Planet Publications, 2nd edition, 1993

Ever since the Lonely Planet's guide to Vietnam exhorted travellers to sample the 'awesome' food prepared by the mute owner of Lac Thahn Restaurant, every mute in Hue seems to have opened a restaurant. What's worse, they're all clustered around the original, so unassuming backpackers, greeted by a stony wall of silence in any of them, could mistakenly think they're in the right place.

Not that this is much of a problem. Since its hearty recommendation, the food has taken a decided turn for the worst. It seems Mr Lac Thahn is too busy chatting with customers, albeit in sign language, and organising tours to the demilitarised zone to bother with cooking anymore.

6.   Equatorial physics

46

Indonesia Handbook
Moon Publications, 4th edition, 1988

You can't accuse Bill Dalton of leaving readers guessing on where he stands on the age-old question of whether you lose your shadow on the equator or not. When describing the equator monument in Bonjol he urges readers to 'pause for a few moments to notice that you've lost your shadow. Following closely like a child all your life, growing from short to long, it suddenly and alarmingly vanishes'. Apart from an unforgivable example of over-writing, Bill is also guilty of getting his equatorial facts wrong. You can stand on the equator all day long most days of the year and not shake your shadow. Only on the two equinoxes will it vanish, and then only briefly around the middle of the day. Thanks to Bill, Bonjol is full of fretting foreigners considering therapy because their shadows didn't disappear.

7.   Da-lat: the Paris of the East

Vietnam: a travel survival kit
Lonely Planet Publications, 2nd edition, 1993

Perhaps the most chastening example of the dangers of guidebook hyperbole. Authors Robert Story and Daniel

Robinson—both Americans incidentally—go into overdrive, describing Da-lat as '... the most delightful city in all of Vietnam. That it was once called 'Le Petit Paris' is a great compliment to the capital of France'.

Not surprisingly, Da-lat doesn't live up to the hype. In fact, it doesn't even get close. The result is a large number of ill-tempered backpackers wandering around Da-lat kicking over market stalls in frustration.

I can only surmise that the authors found some particularly potent mushrooms in the hills around Da-lat before writing this entry.

8. Mr Mohammed Arif, Male

Maldives: a travel survival kit
Lonely Planet Publications, 1st edition, 1990

Anyone who has arrived in the Maldives surrounded by packs of honeymooning Europeans knows that it's not exactly the kind of place that rolls out the welcome mat for scruffy, independent backpackers. That's why it is so reassuring to read the Lonely Planet's assertion that a guy called Mohammed Arif often meets flights to the island and is extremely helpful to independent travellers.

Unfortunately Mr Arif doesn't meet the planes any more. He sends his lackeys instead. Worse still, he's gone upmarket. You'll be whisked away by taxi—your shout, of course—to the Sun Tours offices where the well-dressed Mr Arif, his desk littered with faxes from all corners of Europe and a mobile phone within reach, will try and sell you the most expensive resort accommodation available.

9. Any guidebook that suggests avoiding Maccas

Don't you hate guidebooks that get all high and mighty and suggest that eating a Big Mac while you're travelling is the cultural equivalent of farting in church? I know I do.

What they don't seem to understand is that sometimes a Big Mac or a Whopper is just what you feel like, especially after travelling in the backblocks of Indonesia for months on end. Sure, it's kind of sad that there are more McDonald's in Budapest than opera houses but then that's true of most countries. And besides, in some places like Hong Kong, Macca's is the cheapest meal available short of rummaging through garbage bins with the local bums.

Korea: a travel survival kit
Lonely Planet Publications, 2nd edition, 1985

Described as 'an absolute must' the giant
Buddha in the Popju-sa temple complex in
Sogri-san National Park is the largest
Buddha statue in Korea. So monu-
mental is the structure that Geoff
Crowther described it as 'dominat-
ing' the complex. I arrived after a
shaky seven-hour bus ride from
Seoul to be left distinctly under-
whelmed. The bugger had been
pulled down to be coated with gold
leaf in time for the Seoul Olympics.

48

● ●
Honourable mention: 'Rude Noises' Fact Box
Ethiopia, Eritrea and Djibouti
Lonely Planet Publications, 1st edition, 2000
After unnecessarily telling readers that throughout the African Horn farting is regarded as 'the
height of bad manners', author Frances Linzee
Gordon feels compelled to tell us the Ethiopian
spin on how different nationalities deal with the
issue. Apparently they find the way the Italians will
fart anywhere—and the 'ensuing hilarity'—deeply
shocking. And the French attempts at subterfuge
are regarded as deceitful. Frances' advice? A
quick *yikerta* (excuse me)!
● ●

Chapter 6

PACKING

I don't know about you, but I'm sick and tired of guidebooks telling me to place everything I plan to take travelling on a bed and then put half of it back. For mine, packing is about grabbing what you want, when you want it and shoving it willy-nilly into a suitable receptacle. With that in mind, I offer the following advice.

If there is one thing I should absolutely pack, what is it?

You've probably looked at the music charts and asked yourself what kind of people would buy Mariah Carey and Michael Bolton CDs. Well, when you go travelling you'll meet them. That's why it is absolutely essential that you take a Walkman and your own tapes or discs.

What else should I take?

If you were to believe some guidebooks, you wouldn't go travelling without half the contents of your medicine cabinet in tow. Others insist that we should all be wearing wash-and-wear slacks. I mean, does anyone even know what slacks look like?

To me, packing is a personal thing. If you want to take your detailed 1:250 scale model of the Starship Enterprise when you go trekking in the Himalayas, why shouldn't you be able to? Similarly, if all you want to take are the clothes on your back, so be it—as long as you stand downwind of me.

Still, there are some items I have found particularly useful over the years. They include:

49

- o **Ticket, passport and money:** It's amazing how much more smoothly your travels will go with these three simple items.

- o **At least one set of clothes:** Most major airlines still seem to frown upon nudity.

- o **An umbrella:** Better than a Gor-Tex coat and a fraction of the cost. Also handy for beating off rabid dogs and hotel touts.

- o **A shortwave radio:** Great for catching up on the football scores back home and for checking whether the regional conflict in the country you're about to visit has developed into World War III.

- o **Tampons:** Unavailable in some underdeveloped countries, and a little bulkier than you may be used to in most others. Keenly sought after in black markets and hostels alike.

- o **A Swiss army knife:** I was always quite derisive of backpackers bearing these ubiquitous red beasts until someone gave me one and I found how genuinely useful they are. Terrific for flicking open menacingly when walking back to your hotel after dark in Nairobi.

Is it possible to take too much?

The only time that you have to worry about taking too much is when the airline wants to charge you for excess baggage. At the rates they charge, a pair of extra underpants can work out more expensive than a few ounces of gold.

Anything less than that—and take into account that most airlines will let you get away with 30 kilos—doesn't really matter. The heavier your bag, the quicker you'll lose those troublesome kilos around your midriff.

Is it possible to take too little?

Not really. You can buy pretty much anything you need on the road. Sure, some of the fashions are a little dodgy, and Chinese batteries only last a few seconds, but that's all part of experiencing different cultures, isn't it?

50

What kind of bag should I take?

Once again, a matter of personal taste. Each type of bag has its advantages and disadvantages. I once met a pair of English guys in Colombia using a large wooden coffin to carry their gear in. Weighing more than a small baby elephant, the thing struck me as the height of impracticality. However, they insisted that, apart from having to use hearses instead of taxis, it wasn't any more difficult than lugging around a backpack. They also joked it was great for smuggling out rare antiquities and small amounts of drugs as customs officials were most reluctant to look inside.

What about hard suitcases?

Hard suitcases are useful for sitting on while waiting for railway ticket offices to open or for sheltering behind during an unexpected fire fight. They also seem to come out onto the baggage carousel at airports a good few days before any backpacks on the same flight. However, they are not particularly well-suited to hiking through virgin rainforest.

What about soft backpacks?

Backpacks, on the other hand, while useless during a surprise mortar attack, are a lot easier to sling onto the tops of buses, lug from one full guesthouse to another and break into when you lose the key to your padlock after a night on the piss. They are also more comfortable to sit on while waiting for railway ticket offices to open. The only disadvantage to using a backpack is the lurid colours they come in.

51

Why are backpacks such lurid colours?

It's my bet that backpack manufacturers work in close consultation with taxi drivers and hotel touts from all over the world to create colours that can be seen from a couple of kilometres away, regardless of light and weather conditions. The touts and taxi drivers probably pay the manufacturers a small percentage of their takings as a token of appreciation.

Is there anything I can do to tone down the colour of my backpack?

Some people like to roll their brand new backpack in the dirt or smear it in animal fats in an attempt to dull the synapse-snapping colour scheme. While this is quite effective in altering the pack's hues, it may cause problems when drug sniffer dogs take a liking to your soiled pack's new odour.

When should I pack?

I'm a firm believer in the chaos theory. Therefore I like to pack just as the taxi taking me to the airport arrives. It's a system that has resulted in a few pleasant surprises—like a Lenny Kravitz tape I thought I'd lost—and quite a few blunders. The glow-in-the-dark bedside lamp being the most memorable.

Another benefit of this method is that you often forget basic items like toothpaste, shoes and other items essential to personal hygiene. So when you arrive in a strange and distant land you are immediately forced to venture out and deal with the locals—instead of succumbing to the natural instinct of locking yourself into a room for a couple of days and peeping out through the keyhole.

Should I take gifts?

Sure. It's always a good idea to take a small gift to give as a token of appreciation for the unexpected kindness while travelling—preferably something from your country. This can be a badge, stickpin or even a postcard of your home town. Coming from a country full of exotic and strange animals (not all of which can be found propping up a bar), I also have the option of giving crap like those little cling-on koalas. A Zairian border guard once took one from me in lieu of the $20 bribe he'd originally asked for.

52

In some of the more primitive cultures, the Australian $1 coin also holds some novelty value. The locals are fascinated that a gold-coloured coin can be worth so little.

TOP 10 MOST USELESS THINGS TO PACK

We've all had them. Those little things that we thought would be indispensable but end up spending the entire trip on the bottom of our backpacks. For many, that item is their travelling companion. In the name of human understanding, I've decided to limit this discussion to the following 10 inanimate objects.

1. Washing powder

In many under-developed countries there are people willing to wash, dry and press your clothes for the cost of a Mars Bar. As such, if you take a bag of washing powder away with you, you'll only come back with it six months later scattered throughout the nooks and crannies of your backpack.

A word of warning: Washing powder also seems to excite the interest of customs officers the world over—sometimes to the extent of a cavity search or two.

53

2. Traveller's neck pillow

You know them—those ridiculous boomerang-shaped inflatable pillows that nestle around your neck like a pair of strangling hands.

Two questions: Do they work? And why do grandparents insist on giving them as going away presents?

3. Textbooks/study notes/reports

Why do it to yourself? You're travelling to get away from all these things. You don't need a constant reminder of what you *should* be doing. Besides, a textbook or report will only prove to be a deadweight at the bottom of your backpack, taking up space that could be better used for a souvenir carved salad bowl.

4. Condoms

Don't think for a moment that **NSITT** condones unsafe sex. Quite the contrary! It's just that we've found that packing a six-pack of prophylactics is the surest way of nobbling your chances of finding a little holiday romance. Not to mention robbing yourself and your new-found love of the bonding experience of searching the streets of a strange city for a 24-hour chemist.

5. Trangia/portable gas cooker

Be honest! Do you really want to cook when you could be hoeing into a three-course meal that costs a fraction of the hermetically sealed, freeze-dried gunk you brought along with you? And that's not to mention having to clean the bloody thing afterwards!

There is also a little-mentioned, deadly side-effect of carrying your own cooking gear. A friend of mine had his Trangia searched at gunpoint after it rattled inadvertently at an army checkpoint in Burundi. The guard very nearly pulled the trigger when he found an avocado inside that had been forgotten for six weeks.

6. Those little wheelie things for the bottom of bags

Ever tried using them on a backpack?

7. Universal all-in-one power point adapter

In principle, an adapter that, thanks to the marvels of modern technology, allows you to plug your electrical appliance into any power point anywhere in the world is a fine device. But I've always had two problems with them. One, I found I needed a doctorate in design engineering to work it. Two, once I figured it out, I realised that I didn't have any electrical appliances to plug in anyway.

54

8. Your favourite T-shirt

Sure it's cool—and the first few people who see it will tell you so. But how are you going to feel when it mysteriously changes colour at the hands of the dhobi-wallahs in India or gets torn as you struggle aboard a packed Pelni passenger ship in Indonesia? Best, I think, to put up with the hideous local variety, like the tasteful 'Nha Trang Tourist' T-shirt available in Vietnam, for example. After all, travelling isn't a fashion parade you know!

9. Language phrase book

It's tempting to get yourself a little phrase book, bone up on the appropriate sentence and attempt to speak to the locals in their own tongue. If you're as skilled as me with foreign languages, however, locals will insist that you speak to them in English, even when they can't understand it.

55

10. A money belt

Why make life easy for every hoodlum, thief and con man within three kilometres by keeping all your worldly possessions strapped around your midriff? Leave them in your hotel room where the hotel manager can help himself to them.

56

Chapter 7

HEALTH

Listen to any doctors or read any guidebook and you'd think the world was a bubbling, boiling cauldron of disease just waiting to lay you low and spoil your holiday. It is. But if you take the following sage words into account you should be able to survive—just.

Should I get fit before I go travelling?

Why waste all that money and effort getting into shape before you go? Treat the earth as the world's biggest gym and travelling as the most interesting way of working out in it. A couple of days lugging an over-sized pack from one flea-infested hostel to another and you'll be in the best shape you've ever been in.

What are the greatest dangers to my health while travelling?

Well, apart from civil strife and men wielding big sharp knives, you should also be wary of the following threats:

o **Alcohol:** Freed of the constraints of study and work, many travellers overindulge in the local brew. The wildly inaccurate and varying alcohol levels don't help matters either.

o **Airline food:** Its pallid and unappealing appearance is an accurate indication of the parlous state it will leave you in.

57

o **Malaria:** No matter what anti-malarial drug you choose, you can be certain that the mozzies will have well and truly built up an immunity to it by the time you reach their swampy neck of the woods.

- o **Local buses:** It's not only the buses in the Third World that are scandalously unroadworthy. The drivers are in pretty bad shape too. Most are either drunk, stoned or suicidal.

- o **Cholera,** yellow fever, typhoid fever, meningitis, hepatitis A, hepatitis B, hepatitis C, tetanus, polio, rabies, sleeping sickness, bilharzia, dysentery, giardiasis, tropical ulcers, AIDS, gonorrhoea, syphilis, Japanese encephalitis, dengue fever... I think you get the picture.

Should I get vaccinations before I go?

It all depends where you are going and the style in which you're planning to travel. If you're going to Europe on a hermetically-sealed business trip, probably not. Anywhere else though and you probably should.

Of course, it also depends on your normal lifestyle and eating habits. You may have already come across some of the more notorious diseases and built up an immunity to them. Most college and university students have usually built up an immunity to most major diseases by the end of their first year. Everyone else, however, should consider getting jabs.

But I'm afraid of needles...

Well, you're in trouble then. If you want to travel to the Third World—and I include New York in that—and you want to be properly immunised, you're going to end up feeling like a human pincushion.

From hepatitis to rabies, from typhoid fever and tetanus through to Japanese encephalitis, there's a shot for everything these days. Just make sure they stamp them all in one of those yellow International Certificates of Vaccination for you. You don't want to endure all that pain and suffering only to go through it all again at an isolated border post where the guard's idea of hygiene is wiping the needle clean on his grubby uniform between each shot.

58

You'll be pleased to know, however, that not all vaccinations need to be injected. The one for polio, for example, is taken orally. A friend of mine didn't realise this and after a particularly gruesome bout of injections fainted when the doctor informed him that the polio vaccination was to be given under the tongue. There was a positive side-effect though. When he was finally revived he was rewarded with a sticker of a cartoon kangaroo saying, 'I was good at the doctor's today'.

Should I take my own medical kit?

An unfortunate side-effect of the spread of medical centres specifically catering for the traveller has been the
emergence of the medical kit as a product.

Realising that the next month's payment on the Maserati
isn't going to be paid by a couple of tetanus shots and
the odd polio vaccine, these centres have come up with
the brilliant idea of bundling all their slow-moving medicines into a plastic box with a red cross on it and selling
them as 'purpose built' medical kits. With names like
'The Out Of Africa Pack' and 'The Adventurer's Pack' (it's
the one with condoms), they cost a fortune and are full
of useless stuff like electrodes and leeches.

59

Rather than spend your entire holiday budget on one of these kits, you'll
find that it is far more economical and practical to make up your own
medical kit. That way you can take into account your own medical history, susceptibilities and cough syrup habit.

For what it's worth, I take a tube of Savlon for cuts and abrasions, a six-
pack of Panadol for headaches, and a tube of Beroccas for everything
else. Usually, only the Beroccas get used.

What about syringes?

With the spread of AIDS and the parlous state of the public health system
in some countries, a lot of travellers
have started taking their own syringes
when they travel to places like Africa,
Asia and the United Kingdom. If you
have a problem with a doctor injecting
you with a syringe that has been used
several hundred times before, you
should too.

If you do, you should be aware of the problems syringes cause on some
border crossings. Even if you have a letter of authorisation from your
doctor explaining that the syringes are meant for life-threatening medical
reasons, chances are the customs officer on duty that day can't read
English. He'll be convinced that the syringes are meant for more nefari-
ous purposes and will spend the afternoon ransacking your bag and ori-
fices looking for proof.

Is prevention better than a cure for diarrhoea as well?

That's certainly the line peddled by most guidebooks and medical authorities. They argue that if you're careful about what you eat and drink you can avoid most of the more common ailments like diarrhoea and dysentery.

60

There are flaws with this theory though. For one thing, if you avoided eating and drinking everything they suggest, you'd starve.

And then there's that dubious piece of advice that you shouldn't eat food from a food stall where the owner looks sickly. Guidebooks assume that it's because he's been eating his own food. If I'd taken this advice I would have gone hungry every night of my childhood.

What is Bali Belly?

Bali Belly is just another name, albeit a little more alliterative and colourful, for good old fashioned diarrhoea. Other equally quaint names include the Rangoon Runs, Montezuma's Revenge, Delhi Belly and the rather more direct The Shits. The preponderance of such names indicates the affectionate regard travellers have for this particular ailment.

Can I *really* avoid diarrhoea?

I have a personal theory—totally unsupported by any data and based only on my own empirical observations—that diarrhoea is in fact a psychosomatic disease. People read so much about the disease that they become convinced that no matter what they eat, drink or do, they will get it—and they do. I once travelled to Bali with a girl who got a dose of the runs on the plane over. She hadn't even touched the airline food.

What about drinking bottled water? That would help, wouldn't it?

Yes. Tap water is perhaps the greatest threat to your health not because of a contaminated water source, but rather the dubious state of the plumbing in most of the places you're likely to be staying in or eating at.

But beware! Some bottled water is not all that it appears to be. Those little kids who grab the plastic bottle out of your hand just as you finish aren't collecting them for the fun of it. They are in the employ of a huge, multi-national recycling concern that refills those bottles with the same tap water that you've been trying to avoid.

The only way to protect yourself from this scam is to examine your bottled water carefully before you buy it. A broken seal is not a good sign, nor is brown, murky colouring or small fish.

I hear that diarrhoea is one of the greatest things about travelling. Is that true?

A lot of people only focus on the unpleasant sides of Montezuma's Revenge. They remember the hours spent squatting over an unsanitary hole in the ground or the severe stomach cramps that convinced them they were about to die. They forget about the more positive and life-affirming aspects of 'having The Shits'.

For one, it's a great conversation starter. Nothing breaks the ice in an awkward social situation while you're travelling better than an offhand 'Gees, something's gone through me like a ton of bricks'. Almost immediately your silent companions will come over all lively and animated, relating tales of their own bowel movements. Even the most prim and proper travellers will regale you with the kinds of details usually reserved for medical journals. Chances are you'll find that their silence was caused by the strict concentration demanded of them by a current bout of the dreaded lurgy.

How can I get rid of diarrhoea?

If you must, most doctors, health authorities and hypochondriacs advise that you avoid fatty foods and eat only dry biscuits and rice. Anyone who has travelled throughout the Third World knows that this is impossible. Absolutely everything is cooked in fat, usually a number of times and over a number of weeks. Any dry biscuits you may find have long passed their use-by date, which in most cases is in Roman numerals or hieroglyphics. And you've probably long reached the stage where if you have to eat another bowl of rice you'll walk into a rice-threshing factory and do something you rather wish you hadn't.

It is best, I think, just to keep eating what you feel like—although in some countries that is a challenge in itself. It won't help your affliction, but it will stop you feeling miserable and depressed. Just make sure you're within sprinting distance of a toilet. While I was in Kigali in Rwanda I made the embarrassing mistake of overestimating the capacity of my bowels after a particularly fine French meal at the Café Étoile. Stepping out into the crisp evening air I was convinced that I could make it back to the hostel I was staying in quite comfortably. Halfway through the final 500-metre dash I found out I was wrong.

What about drugs?

After spending a number of evenings becoming intimately familiar with the nuances of Egyptian plumbing you may be tempted to turn to drugs to help you get through it. Anyone who has been afflicted knows that this is a condition that demands the highest standards of discipline, timing and accuracy. It is therefore best suffered straight.

No, I mean drugs as in medicine

Oh, like Imodium or Lomotil? Hmmm. That's a tricky one. Personally, I think it's best to leave it to your body to sort out. There's a good reason for your body trying to flush itself out with such vigour. Once it figures out how to beat this particular bug, the chances of you getting it again are minimised. Confuse it with some kind of drug and it will welcome every known disorder this side of the equator. What's the point of having an immune system if you're not going to use it?

62

Are there any countries I can travel to without worrying about my health?

Not really. It's just that in different regions you'll have different things to worry about. In Asia, Africa, the Middle East and South America, your concerns will be physical ones like: 'Am I going to survive the arduous 48-hour journey to the nearest witchdoctor?' In Europe and

North America, they'll be financial ones. Like how you'll pay for an ambulance ride that costs more than flying on the Concorde.

Any final words on health?

Yes. Be careful of buying medicines made in India and Asia. Some of the less scrupulous pharmaceutical companies use these countries as a testing ground for drugs the authorities have banned back home. Take an antibiotic bought in Pakistan and you could wake up with an extra digit.

63

You should also be careful of the diet pills sold on Ko Pha-Ngan on the night of the Full Moon party. Rather than curbing your appetite, they make you jump up and down on the same spot, making big boxes and little boxes with your hands all night.

TOP 10 TRAVELLERS' AILMENTS

Despite miraculous advances in tropical and exotic medicine, there are still some travelling diseases that you simply can't immunise against. They are strange afflictions of the mind, with prevention the only cure and vigilance your only ally. This is your guide to 10 of the most deadly.

1. Exaggeritis

Particularly prevalent amongst travellers who have been on the road for years on end. Symptoms include the sufferer making wildly improbable claims about where they have been, what they have seen and how much they have spent. While not communicable, if someone starts telling you that they travelled on 53 cents a day by sleeping on park benches and recycling their own urine, you should give them a wide berth—if only for your own sanity.

2. The Cultural Emulation Syndrome

Also known as 'Going Native', this is when a traveller starts adopting the social, dress and eating habits of the country they are visiting. It is particularly prevalent in India, South East Asia and South America, understandably rare in Switzerland. Usually clears up of its own accord when the sufferer is confronted with the reality of going home, though can persist indefinitely in all environments.

64

3. The Cultural Enhancement Syndrome

A strange disease that leads otherwise normal individuals to adopt the nationalistic stereotypes of their country of birth with vigour. In its extreme form it can lead to sufferers invading a small neighbouring country or, at the very least, ruining a once tranquil tropical paradise. Miraculously clears up when the afflicted's country endures a humiliating defeat in an international sporting event.

4. Inflamed Spirituality

Symptoms include the appearance of a fixed beatific smile and a sudden conversion to vegetarianism. Also induces the sudden realisation of the importance of a blue-faced god with eleven arms and legs in the modern Western lifestyle.

5. Constipated Payment Disorder

Where the afflicted traveller baulks at paying the asking rate for an item, even though they would quite happily pay ten times the price for the same thing back home. Also known as having a 'Haggling Hernia'. You could try paying for them, but you risk getting a lecture about it not being about money but the 'principle'.

6. Obsessive Junk Food Craving

Often the result of an unfamiliar and unfulfilling diet for months on end. Symptoms include a psychotic obsession for a particular brand of biscuit or potato crisp. If unchecked, can lead to irrational behaviour such as scouring substandard supermarkets for the said item or catching the first plane home to pig out on it. Less dramatic treatment is adding a little tomato sauce to your rice or ugali for a change, or splashing out and visiting Maccas.

7. Vacational Vocation Amnesia

Ever noticed that when you're travelling everyone you meet seems to have glamorous careers? They're all either writers, artists, actors or have wealthy parents. No one admits to being a bank teller or a parking officer.

65

Like Exaggeritis, this malady is often cured when the sufferer meets someone who really does work for that particular ad agency, publishing company or art gallery.

8. Exaggerated English Pronunciation Disorder

Prevalent in countries where English is not widely understood. Sufferers find themselves speaking abnormally loudly and slowly to ticket sellers, waiters and hostel managers. Beware of possible delusionary side effects. Severe sufferers believe that the person staring blankly at them actually understands what they are saying.

9. Pack Stoop

Caused by lugging an over-heavy backpack from one full hostel to another. Seems to get worse towards the end of a trip when packs are generally loaded with ridiculously heavy souvenirs for friends and families. A couple of days travelling in a second-class sleeper on Indian trains has been known to help.

10. Hyper-empathy Syndrome

This is a most serious disease. The afflicted feel an overwhelming urge to 'connect' with local people and their problems. Symptoms include solemn nodding (usually with a knitted brow), a caring yet patronising tone of voice, and a tendency to write off antisocial behaviour on the part of the locals as some sort of cross-cultural misunderstanding. Particularly lethal in conjunction with a dose of Exaggerated English Pronunciation Disorder. Should this happen, the most humane thing for everyone involved is to have the poor afflicted traveller put down.

66

Chapter 8

SLEEPING

Finding somewhere to lay your sleepy head at night is the first task you'll have to face when you arrive at your chosen destination. You'll either have a bewildering array of choices or none at all. One thing is certain though. In the **NSITT** world of travel, you're more likely to find a cockroach on your pillow than a complimentary mint.

Should I take the first room I find?

Yes. Any seasoned backpacker knows that the first room you look at will always be the best, if for no other reason than it saves you trudging around a strange town looking at rooms you normally wouldn't put your grandmother in.

Similarly, after you've settled into your room and go out to get something to eat, it is inevitable that you'll find an establishment that is cleaner, cheaper and quieter right next door.

How can I tell if a place is a bona-fide backpacker establishment?

The most obvious sign, I guess, is the presence of bona-fide backpackers and a squadron of local Lotharios trying it on with them. Other telltale signs to look for include:

o   *Safety: non-existent.* In any decent backpacker establishment you should be able to immediately notice at least half a dozen different ways for you to be trapped and killed during a fire or natural disaster.

67

o   *Cleanliness: optional.* If the sheets have been washed in the last decade, the establishment is not often used by backpackers.

In fact, you could well be the first, and after you're gone they'll refuse to take any more.

o **Security: negligible.** Windows should be easily entered from the street and the door should show signs of being regularly kicked in.

o **Staff: shifty.** The manager of the establishment should be helpful and eager to please, with a lascivious edge. If you're a guy, you should get an uneasy feeling that your valuables are in danger. If you're a girl, you should feel concerned about your honour.

o **Location: appalling.** You should be able to step out from your backpacker establishment onto a railway line, a freeway overpass or a gangland shooting.

o **Bedbugs: voracious.** In a real backpacker establishment they are trained to attack instantly.

o **Guests: frightening.** Ideally, they will look like the kind of people you cross the street to avoid back home.

o **Price: unfathomable.** If you get the feeling you are being ripped off, especially if the amount you're paying is only a few cents or so, you know that you're in a fair dinkum backpacker establishment.

What should I look for in a room?

I was going to be smart and say four walls and a roof, but in some hotels I've stayed in, even those were optional. One particular establishment in Macau—I won't name it as my negligence claim against them still hasn't been resolved—virtually demolished itself while I slept there.

68

Still, there are a few things you should look for in a room, even if it's only to negotiate a better price. Pillows should be hard, lumpy and preferably stained. Sheets should be torn, crusty and impossible to determine original colour or pattern. Any toilet, either in your room or down the hall, should either leak constantly or refuse to flush.

Is there a single most important thing a room should have?

A good exit. Not in case of a fire, but for when fellow backpackers take their boots off.

Should I stay in a place recommended in a guide-book?

I am yet to stay in a place that gets the best write-up in the guidebook I'm using. Much to the delight of the owners, places that receive a hearty write-up in one of the guidebooks seem to be perpetually full—so much so that many of the owners have to start another hotel to take the overflow. The New Kenya Lodge in Nairobi now has the New Kenya Lodge Annex. And the owner of the hotel simply known as Guesthouse 72 at 72 Bui Vien Street in Ho Chi Minh City, Vietnam, now operates guesthouses at 70, 68, 54 and 37.

You could try being perverse and go directly to the hotel or guesthouse that gets the worst write-up. But even that doesn't always work. A lot of people won't stay anywhere unless it is mentioned in a guidebook, no matter how unflattering or frightening that mention may be.

What about just going to a known backpacker ghetto and seeing what turns up?

69

Good idea. Every city where backpackers congregate has its own precinct where the Birkenstock and cut-off jeans brigade hang out. In Bangkok it's Khao San Road. In Istanbul it's Sultanahmet. In Sydney, it's Victoria Street, Kings Cross. Wander the streets wearing a backpack in any of these areas and you're bound to be accosted by some slovenly backpacker offering you a room. Even if you're not, chances are you'll stumble across some little unheralded joint that is both friendly and cheap.

A word of warning though. Hotels and guesthouses change their names more often than they change their sheets. That little unheralded place you discover could simply be an establishment that was slagged off under a different name.

How can I save money on accommodation?

Short of wandering around at night and sleeping under bushes during the day, not easily. You could try catching overnight buses and trains everywhere, but if you plan to return to your university, job or loved one in a fit state to perform it's best to give this method of saving money a miss.

What about staying with friends?

I have a rather biblical approach to this question. Only stay with those whom you would happily have stay at your place—and even then only stay for a couple of days.

I don't deny that it's tempting when you arrive in a fiendishly expensive place to look up someone you may have met once and impose yourself upon them. Just don't do it. The money you save will be extracted from you over and over again as first that person reciprocates with a lengthy visit to your home, and then their family, their friends and, finally, the person they struck up a conversation with on the train to work. After the success of the 2000 Olympics in Sydney, it's something I have to be particularly careful about.

70

What about staying with family?

A very wise man once said you can choose your friends, but you can't choose your family. What most people don't realise is that he coined the phrase after staying with his relos on a trip to England.

Should I let a tout take me to a hotel?

What do you need more—your money or your sleep?

If money's tight, avoid the little buggers like the plague. They'll take you to the hotel that offers them the highest commission with a determination rarely seen outside Olympic sporting events. It is not unknown for touts to walk straight by perfectly good places with plenty of beds to spare, simply because they know they can get a couple of extra rupiah at a joint on the other side of town.

However, if you're tired, dirty and agitated, that nagging little tout could be your quickest route to a bed for the night. Sure, you'll have to pay double the going rate, but what price an extra couple of hours sleep?

What about taxi drivers?

If anything, taxi drivers are worse than touts. While touts may be tempted to give up finding you a room in a hotel that offers the most ridiculously high commission if it gets too hot or too difficult, taxi drivers have an incentive to keep going. As they drag you from one end of town to another, assuring you that the hotel that looked perfectly empty was in fact booked out by a busload of conventioneering toilet brush salesmen, they are content in the knowledge that the meter is ticking away quite merrily.

Why do some hotels refuse to take backpackers?

If someone turned up on your doorstep looking like you do when you go travelling, would you let them wallow in your clean sheets and mess up your toilet with their guts racked by diarrhoea? I didn't think so!

If I meet someone special, will I have trouble taking them back to my room?

Most hotels and guesthouses have accepted—some grudgingly, others admiringly—the loose morals of backpackers. So you're not likely to face any problems on moral grounds or have to go through the rigmarole of registering as husband and wife except maybe in a few of the more fundamentist countries and some of the southern states of America.

71

The only problems you're likely to face are financial ones. Hotel owners see an extra person entering a room and figure that they should pay. I witnessed a very violent argument between an Australian guy and a hotel owner who couldn't quite comprehend the Aussie's line of reasoning that he shouldn't have to pay extra just because 'he got lucky'.

What about in a hostel dorm?

Of course, many of the dorms in YHA and private hostels are unisex these days, with guys and girls from all over the world sharing body odours together. It's a free-and-easy scene where folk get around in nought but a sarong and no one bats an eyelid. That doesn't mean you can bring your new-found lover back to your dorm for a bit of horizontal folk dancing though. With the sad and sorry state of most hostel bunks, you'd end up keeping the whole dorm awake.

Will staying in a dump bring me in closer contact with the locals?

Many backpackers mistakenly reason that by staying in a less than salubrious establishment they are seeing the real side of the particular country they are visiting. What they fail to realise is that these types of establishments become backpacker hostels and guesthouses because the locals refuse to use them.

What about staying in a local's home?

In many countries, particularly in Eastern Europe, you will be approached by people offering to rent you a room in their house. Sometimes this can prove to be a rewarding and enlightening experience, providing a unique insight into the lifestyle and aspirations of the ordinary folk of the country you are visiting. Most of the time, however, it simply results in a long night flicking through photo albums of people you don't know and listening to stories you don't understand.

72

TOP 10 SHITHOLES

You may be wondering why I am not listing all the wonderful places I have stayed in—the places where I have been moved by the spectacular scenery or touched by the generosity of the people. Well, for some reason, it's the worst places that I have slept in that I hold the fondest memories. Call me perverse, but here are 10 of the worst/best.

1. Borneo Homestay, Banjarmasin, Indonesia, August 1991

Perched precariously over a particularly grimy, slimy canal in the humid hellhole that is Banjarmasin, the Borneo Homestay appears to be disintegrating before your very eyes. Unfortunately, it is only an optical illusion. Inside, each crudely partitioned room boasts a bed with mattresses soggy enough to grow rice on and a mosquito net with more holes than OJ Simpson's defence. The whole experience is topped off at midnight when the Homestay's long-term residents—a family of rather large rats—return after a long day scavenging through rubbish and scurry along the partition. If you're lucky they'll make it to the other side without falling onto your pillow. I wasn't.

73

2. Busha Beni Lodge, Beni, Zaire, January 1992

If it wasn't for the wallpaper, the 'Busha' would be just another African 'cube'. The style and colour of the pattern suggests that the wallpaper was put up in the seventies—though in Africa that's not always a good indication. More importantly, due to the humidity the glue has never quite dried, so that under the weight of a particularly hefty mosquito or gecko it peels and falls stickily across the face of unsuspecting guests. I spent my night there fending off the unwanted advances of a particularly lurid strip of purple swirled wallpaper.

3. Hotel Felix, Quito, Ecuador, April 1992

Nestled at the bottom of a cobbled street in the old part of Quito, the Hotel Felix has the unfortunate distinction of being near the junction of the street where all the hookers hang out the windows and the one where all the drunks rolling home take a piss. The owners try to compensate those unfortunate enough to get the rooms overlooking the streets with flower boxes.

4. Club du Lac Tanganyika, Bujumbura, Burundi, November 1991

Don't be fooled by the name. Club du Lac ain't no Club Med. It's just a cluster of dusty boat sheds down by Lake Tanganyika, where wealthy ex-pats once kept their boats. The place does provide shelter though for backpackers who have unwittingly walked into one of Bujumbura's frequent massacres. I spent three days curled up in an old wooden runabout that hadn't been used since the Belgians left.

5. Ilknur Pansiyon, Istanbul, Turkey, April 1994

The owners of this hostel, the legendary 'Tache and his wife, are, I believe, certifiably mad. I guess that, due to the chronic overcrowding of Turkish asylums they have been allowed to open a backpacker hostel.

The best thing about the Ilknur is the price—A$2.50 a night at last count—and the views of the Bosphorus from the dorms upstairs. The worst thing is that since the gas heater blew up in the guests' bathroom, singeing the hair of the unfortunate backpacker using it at the time, you have to use the 'Tache's bathroom downstairs. Scary thought!

6. Mirador Mansion, Hong Kong, July 1995

What you've got to realise is that the Hong Kong Chinese have a totally different understanding of the meaning of the word 'mansion' than you probably do. To them, a mansion is a crumbling tower block with lifts that never work, stairwells that double as a garbage tip and as many people crammed in as is inhumanely possible.

74

On my last visit to Hong Kong I stayed in a room here where I had to take a number to breathe out. The cramped conditions proved an effective crowd control measure, however, when the police raided the joint at 4 am looking for illegal immigrants. The cop's command of 'Don't move!' seemed a little superfluous.

75

7. More Than Ways hostel, Budapest, Hungary, March 1994

When the touts from the More Than Ways hostel jump you at Keleti Railway Station they seduce you with stories of the great bar and all the other travellers you'll meet. What they rather conveniently forget to tell you is that the bar is open 24 hours a day and that your room is right above it. Nor do they warn you that the only time you're likely to meet your fellow travellers is as they throw up into the basin you were just about to clean your teeth in.

8. Sunray's Lodge, Nairobi, Kenya, January 1992

Situated on the wrong side of Tom Mboya Street, just opposite the fire station, Sunray's Lodge does have a few things going for it. For one thing, it is one of the few places in Nairobi with constant hot water. And the curtains are made of material featuring lions, giraffes and zebras. What you've got to decide is whether it's worth taking your life into your hands when you walk back after sunset.

9. Friendship Lodge, Banaue, the Philippines, August 1989

The rice terraces around Banaue have been called the eighth wonder of the world, but stay at any of the hotels clustered at the bottom of the muddy, rutted road leading from the town and the only wondering you'll do is what the hell you are doing there. I stayed at the Friendship Lodge, a rather seedy establishment with walls so thin I could hear a randy Swedish couple doing what randy Swedish couples do all night long. I could have coped if the female Swede hadn't taken the opportunity to practice her vowels as well. You try sleeping while a mattress squeaks to the sounds of 'a, e, i, o, u'!

76

Situated on the idyllic east coast of this fabled island, Bwejuu is promoted as an untouched paradise. And, thanks to the difficult road across to the other side of the island, it largely is. An unfortunate side-effect to all this is that you can get stranded. A friend and I got stuck there for ten days. In desperation, we turned to the Tanzanian Scotch, a rather perilous brew coloured a disturbing shade of orange. Things got really bad when the hotel ran out of coke and we had to mix it with Fanta.

●●●●●●●●●●●●●●●●●●●●●●●●●●

Postscript: Bwejuu Bungalows, April 2001

Call me a glutton for punishment or an incurable nostalgic, but on a recent trip to Zanzibar I returned to the East Coast and stayed once more at the Bwejuu Bungalows. Now under new management, the orange Scotch is no longer available and, although new extensions have been built, the place seems to be in a worse state than my last visit. Travellers looking for sun, sand and reasonably-priced accommodation are better off trying the places that have sprung up around Nungwe Beach instead.

●●●●●●●●●●●●●●●●●●●●●●●●●●

Chapter 9

EATING

It can make your trip or it can cut it short. It can bring you closer to the locals or it can widen the gulf. It's something you have to have even when sometimes you rather wish you didn't. This is your stomach-turning guide to the staff of life—food.

Should I be wary of eating while I'm travelling?

Listen to some people and you wouldn't open your mouth at all. They argue that each meal put before you has the potential to lay you low and spoil your whole trip. Unless you're going away for nothing more than a couple of hours, this isn't really practical. You're going to have to eat something. Just expect to be gastronomically disappointed.

77

Is there anything I should avoid in particular?

If you can manage to avoid the following items, you should be able to keep major disappointment at bay—at least for a couple of minutes anyway.

o   **Bread:** In Asia it's too sweet. In Africa, it's unrecognisable. And outside of America the closest thing to rye you'll find is the grin on the face of the guy flogging it to you.

o   **Icecream in the tropics:** Unlike anything you have ever seen or tasted. Given that refrigeration is still an inexact science in many parts of the world, this is hardly surprising.

o   **Dairy products in Asia:** Probably has something to do with the fact that dairy cows don't really adapt well to the tropical heat.

o   **Biscuits:** If they're meant to be sweet, they'll be salty. If they're meant to be salty, they'll be sweet. And regardless of the flavour they are meant to be, they will be long past their use-by date anyway.

o   ***Pizza in Italy:*** Nowhere near as good as back home and infinitely more expensive. It is believed that Italian restaurant owners can put their kids through college on the proceeds of just one Super Supreme.

o   ***Anything still moving in China:*** That is, mostly everything you will be served.

o   ***Anything you can't readily identify:*** This is a problem you may also face in most university cafeterias.

Of course, there are many foods that seem okay at first but become tiresome by the nineteenth straight time you eat them. Rice in Indonesia is a perfect example of this.

Should I eat from food stalls?

Hey, why not? If you want to add a little adventure and excitement to your trip this is probably the quickest and easiest way to do it.

After all, their standards of hygiene may be low, but so are their prices. They've got no overheads to speak of, staff costs are minimal and, unlike McDonald's, the savings are passed on directly to you. Hence you can stuff yourself for a matter of cents.

78

Of course, there are the drawbacks. In order to make some money from their pathetic enterprise, stallholders will often buy the crappiest cuts of meat and the saddest looking vegetables. Then, in an attempt to make them the slightest bit palatable, they will boil or fry these ingredients to within an inch of their nutritional life.

How should I pick a restaurant?

As most backpacker restaurants are little more than glorified street stalls, apply the same rules as you would in picking the street stall of your choice. Check the condition of the chef. Look at the state of the food. Sniff the ingredients for any disagreeable odours.

If that doesn't help, turn your attention to the diners instead. Are they lively and gregarious? Or are they sullenly playing with their food? Are they heartily attacking their meal? Or are they scraping it under the table for the local dogs to turn up their noses at?

If all that sounds a little too hard, just toss a coin.

Should I check the hygiene standards of the place I am eating in?

79

There are two things you really don't want to see in life. One is your parents having sex. The second is the state of the kitchen in restaurants catering for backpackers.

What should I do if I can't read the menu?

A lot of guidebooks suggest that if you can't read a menu you should quickly survey what others around you are eating and point to the meal that takes your fancy. This is fine in theory but in reality presents two practical hurdles. One is making the waiter understand that it is the meal you're interested in and not the diner, and the second is that you can actually see something that you could conceivably digest.

Whatever you do, don't just take a gamble and point to something at random on the menu. It is inevitable that it will be something that you would never think of eating back home or that the health authorities would even let you eat.

What about getting a picnic lunch together?

Who amongst us hasn't dreamed of getting a bit of brie and a bundle of baguettes and heading off into the French countryside for a picnic with a loved one? Charming and cheap, it is perhaps the ultimate travel fantasy, particularly if the said loved one turns out to be Elle Macpherson or Brad Pitt.

Those of us who have indulged will admit that it is one of the highlights of travelling. However, when picnicking becomes a matter of survival and you're forced to eat bread and cheese every day out of necessity, it soon loses its charm.

Should I eat the local delicacy?

Hmmm. Tricky question. It could be argued that by consuming the local delicacy you will quickly gain a valuable insight into the culture you are visiting. In my experience, however, the thing it brings you in contact with more immediately is the intricacies of a particular country's plumbing.

Should you feel the need to indulge—or feel that your life is in danger if you don't—remember this simple rule: avoid eating anything that also appears in the country's coat of arms.

What about eating with the locals?

You must realise that in many countries they don't have the luxury of the local supermarket. In fact, most are scratching out a meagre existence from a harsh and unforgiving land. They therefore have to eat basically whatever they can get their hands on.

Hence they don't leave anything to waste, so when you sit down to a meal with a local family you'll find yourself eating parts of animals that you would ordinarily baulk at giving to your cat. I was presented a meal in Siberut, Indonesia, one night that had chicken claws sticking out vertically. To the locals it was a delicacy and they regarded it as a great honour. As I smiled weakly and made pathetic attempts to look like I was enjoying it, they were licking their lips enviously.

Of course, this weird conundrum can often work in your favour. I visited a small fishing village in Kalimantan, Indonesia and was honoured with a meal with the head chief. While everyone else was savouring the can of Spam especially opened for the occasion, I was tucking into prawns the size of cats. The locals ate them every day as part of their staple diet and were sick of them.

What should I know about eating with my hands?

For many first-time travellers the most disturbing thing about travelling to foreign climes is the strange eating methods of the locals. The most alarming is the habit in many Asian and African countries of tossing aside the knives and forks and even the chopsticks to eat with one's hands.

81

Of course, in some university and college dining halls this is common practice so travellers from these august establishments will have little problem assimilating. Those more delicate amongst us, however, should remember the following simple rules. One, never use your left hand. In many countries, your left hand is the equivalent of a six-pack of Sorbent. Two, never shake hands with your mouth full.

How will I know if a meal has disagreed with me?

Any side effects of a poor meal while you are travelling are pretty much instantly apparent. If there's anything dodgy about that vindaloo you've just had, you'll be making a long-distance call on the porcelain telephone within minutes. Of course, this has its benefits. The stuff is out of your system before it can cause any long-term problems. Unlike the heavily processed crap you eat back home, it can take decades for the carcinogenic effects to kick in.

Should I take along something to cook my own food then?

Unless you have a special medical condition that precludes you from eating anything salty, fatty or sweet, it's probably not worth your while. No matter where you go in the Third World you will find someone willing to knock up a meal for a few cents.

Having said that, it's probably not a bad idea to take a small gas cooker along if you're planning to visit Japan or Scandinavia. With the price of even the most basic grocery items in these countries you'll be glad you took it along.

Handy Hint: Freshly caught squirrel is a lot more appetising when it's cooked.

Should I eat Italian in China and vice versa?

In short, no. The lasagne you order in Shanghai will taste and look like a sloppy dumpling. And the chow mien you order in Florence will bear an uncanny resemblance to spaghetti bolognaise.

The only time you should be tempted to eat foreign cuisine in a country other than the dish's country of origin is when there is a large ethnic community living there. They know how to cook it and what it should look and taste like. In fact, in some countries like Australia, where the raw ingredients are good and cheap, the ethnic chefs can make the food better than in the country it originally came from. But maybe that's because their working visa depends on it.

What if I get homesick for a meal from my country?

In some places that won't even be a problem. A strange phenomenon is the ready abundance of your nation's favourite dish in popular package tour destinations. For example, in Majorca, English folk on a five-day excursion from Blighty are able to dine on good old English fish and chips. Similarly, Aussies up in Bali for the week can tuck into a traditional Aussie roast dinner. They can return home with their eating habits unchallenged and unchanged.

Get a little further a field, however, and you'll have to give up any hope of finding something that even vaguely resembles your favourite meal back home. Of course, that's something you'll never have to worry about if you're American. You'll find a McDonald's nearly everywhere you go these days.

Is there one food item I should avoid like the plague?

In a word, ugali. Make it your mantra, tattoo it on your forehead, do whatever it takes to avoid it. It is a plain, tasteless mixture of maize and water that leaves you feeling leaden and queasy. Even if that sounds like half the meals you knock up for yourself back home, believe me, this is much worse. It is a foul, horrid concoction that even the 'authentic' African restaurants back home refuse to serve.

Any last words of advice for vegetarians?
I hope you like rice.

T0P 10
GREATEST
MEALS EVER

They may not have been the most well-presented meals that I have ever had. They may not have been the most delicious or even the most nutritious. But when you're travelling and eating whatever crap you can afford—or even get your hands on—such trifling matters are all relative anyway. Here are 10 meals that, for whatever reason, stay in my mind as being particularly memorable.

1.   Burger King, Singapore

83

The Whopper wasn't anything extraordinary. In fact, as Whoppers go, the beef patty was a little overdone and they had gone a little heavy on the tomato sauce and mayonnaise. But after six weeks in Kalimantan, Indonesia, eating nothing but rice, I thought it was the best damn meal I had ever had.

2.   Hapa Hapa Restaurant, Lamu, Kenya

Hmmm! A char-grilled tuna steak and an ice-cold pineapple lassi in a huge pint glass. It makes me hungry just thinking about it! Oh, and the view out across the water as ancient dhows floated by was pretty impressive too.

3.   Captain's kitchen, a barge somewhere in Zaire

A couple of years ago I caught a barge down the Zaire River from Kisangani to Kinshasa. The captain told me it would take six days and it took six weeks. My supplies of bruised avocados and stale bread rolls were exhausted by the third day and if it hadn't been for the kindly captain's wife I could well have starved. Each night she brought me a bowl of fish soup and some crusty bread to dip into it. It was watery and tasteless, but after a day staring out at a monotonous wall of jungle, it had its charms.

4. Kebab stall near the Blue Mosque, Istanbul, Turkey

Unlike most of the kebab men in Istanbul, Ahmed believes in only using the best quality cuts. That's why he packs his spit full of succulent chicken breast fillets. Grab one of his chicken kebabs on the way to the light and sound show at the Blue Mosque, get him to put a little of his special yoghurt on it and it will indeed be a religious experience.

5. Hotel Dhanbuma, Male, the Maldives

Tucked behind a pair of shuttered saloon doors, the Hotel Dhanbuma remains undiscovered by Italian honeymooners on day trips to Male from their resorts—which is a good thing really. It means that the curry puffs, fish cakes and cornucopia of other Maldivian treats laid out before you on plastic plates to pick from at will remain delicious and affordable.

6. Carnivores, Nairobi, Kenya

There's something obscene about paying $25 for as much roast game as you can eat. Zebra, antelope, ostrich and the occasional elephant knuckle—chances are it's turning on the spit waiting for you to sample it. But after a couple of weeks of Kenyan cuisine you won't even care. This establishment is right next door to the Nairobi National Park where the chef fights with the local pride of lions for the freshest supplies.

7. Crepe House Uni, Tokyo, Japan

The first day I started work at Uni Public Relations in Tokyo they gave me a wad of free vouchers for a fast food crepe house they were handling. As I had not eaten for several weeks due to dire financial circumstances the vouchers were much appreciated and immediately redeemed. As I bit into that first crepe—a jumbo salad crepe if I remember rightly—angels sang and the heavens parted. I guess that's what delirium does to a guy.

8. Nonics, Nairobi, Kenya

In some places it's the food that makes the difference. In others it's the staff. At Nonics, just on the right side of Tom Mboya Street, it is Gloria the surly waitress that makes dining there such a memorable experience. Their motto is 'Let's Talk Food', something that obviously wasn't decided upon in close consultation with Gloria. Her snarling countenance and ability to get even the simplest order wrong, made dining at Nonics a totally unforgettable experience. Well, her and the nonstop Phil Collins *Live in Berlin* video.

9. Fatty's Place, Bam, Iran

Fatty is an Iranian woman who opens her house to Westerners. For a few evil American dollars she will let you stay in her house and eat all her food. The food is prepared by her ancient Iranian grandmother, using recipes handed down through the generations. Each meal was delicately spiced and uniformly delicious, and if it is any indication of the meals being eaten by everyone else in the country, probably the reason eating out has never really caught on in Iran.

10. Home St Jean, Kibuye, Rwanda

A five-star location and cooking to match. While everyone else in Kibuye was grumbling through another plate of matoke and ugali, we were enjoying the finest of French Provençale cooking courtesy of a couple of Belgian nuns up in a stone monastery overlooking the spectacular expanses of Lake Kivu.

● ●
Note: Looking through this list you may be tempted into thinking that Africa is the cuisine capital of the world. Far from it! It's just that food there is so uniformly appalling that even a halfway decent meal takes on the countenance of a gastronomic delight. In the world of **NSITT**, fine dining—like everything else—is a relative experience.
● ●

Chapter 10

DRINKING

Finding something to slake a thirst is not a problem facing today's intrepid backpackers. From London and Paris to the forgotten backwaters of Zaire, you'll find someone offering you something to drink. It's just a matter of whether you'll wish you hadn't taken them up on their offer. Regardless, this is your guide to making your trip one that you can almost, kind of, vaguely, remember.

Should I drink on the plane?

God, you're keen aren't you? You're barely out of the country and already you're intent on writing yourself off!

While there is a lot to be said for drinking on a plane—namely, the fact that it's free—there are a lot of other less apparent side effects. For example, if you aren't fortunate enough to get an aisle seat, you could be trapped beside the window holding back a bursting bladder or an irresistible urge to throw up.

And that's not to mention dehydration. The pressurised cabin will mess you up enough already on that count, but add a couple of litres of beer and your skin will start looking like it has been shrink-wrapped and your urine will turn the colour of a Valencia orange.

87

Of course, the question of dehydration is irrelevant if you are flying home to face an unfinished report, an under-researched essay or the wrath of a wronged loved one. You'll need all the fortification you can get. And if it's free, so much the better.

Drinking while travelling: Some handy hints

Like anything with travel, there are a few rules regarding drinking that will stand you in good stead and perhaps save you from waking up in the gutter, in jail or in an unfamiliar bed. Of course, if any of those options tickle your fancy, please feel free to ignore the advice:

o **Avoid drinking anything clear:** Filtered of all natural ingredients, this is alcohol in its purest form and, in many ways, little more than rocket fuel. In fact, in many parts of the former Soviet Union it probably *is* rocket fuel. Strapped for cash, many republics are bottling and selling the stuff as vodka.

88

o **Don't try to outdrink the locals:** Remember that most of the people you'll fall in with as a back-packer are sad individuals leading meaningless, futile lives. They have nothing better to do than sit around all day drinking and have hence built up an incredible tolerance to the stuff. This is particularly a problem in the pubs of the US and Australia.

o **Don't mention the war:** Don't mention the war, an international sporting humiliation or funny traditional customs that involve dressing up in effeminate costumes. People have a tendency to take these things personally after a couple of drinks and may be prepared to go to extreme lengths to defend their country's honour.

o **Carry a piece of paper bearing your name, your hotel and your nationality:** That way, anyone foraging through your pockets as you lay in the gutter will at least know where you should be.

Can I get to know the locals through drinking?

In many places, a shared drink is a way for people to break down barriers and start communicating. There's something special about sipping on a refreshing ale with a kindly local, smiling inanely and nodding at each other. You may not be able to speak each other's language, but after a couple of drinks at least you'll think you do.

Will drinking really bring me closer to the locals?

The only time that drinking will bring you closer to the locals in any kind of meaningful way is when you both pass out on the floor together.

Should I accept free drinks?

89

In your travels, particularly in the more remote corners of the globe, people will offer to buy you drinks. Although you may suspect they may not be able to afford to, to refuse their offer would be unfriendly. Accept their drink, but repay their kindness in some other way. Like staying in their home, for instance.

Is there any time I shouldn't accept a free drink?

Well, it's probably not a good idea to accept a free drink in an Islamic country where it is illegal to drink alcohol. You're probably being set up by the local revolutionary guard who will then call all his mates over to beat you up with big sticks.

If you're really hanging out for some grog in an Islamic country, just visit the Australian Embassy instead. They're bound to have a couple of cases stashed out the back and, in most places, a night of the week when they flog it to desperate backpackers.

What about alcohol-related cons?

There are certainly plenty of those. Con merchants and thieves the world over have long been conversant with the fact that alcohol is the perfect partner for petty larceny and pilfering. A lubricated backpacker is less likely to notice the nimble fingers of a pickpocket than a sober one—or remember much when they're finally sober enough to go to the police.

If you're planning a big night out, it is probably best to leave your valuables in the hotel or hostel you're staying in. That way, you will know it was the manager who stole them.

Have you ever been had, alcoholically speaking?

I'm afraid so. Even the most seasoned of travellers—something I would never claim to be—fall foul of the free drink tricksters of this world.

My moment of shame came in Athens. I was watching the changing of the guard at Syntagma Square, marvelling at the size of the pom-poms, when a guy asked me the time in English. When I answered in English, he looked astounded and asked me to join him for a drink. I accepted and soon found myself following him through a labyrinth of back lanes and alleys to a rather seedy establishment called the 'Foxy Bar'. That should have been my cue to turn and run but instead I entered and found myself buying drinks for every prostitute inside. At least they only made me buy them drinks.

It sounds like I should never accept a drink

Not necessarily. Like everything with travel you've got to go with your instincts. I was once sitting under a tree waiting for a bus in a small village in Tanzania when I was presented with a note by a small child. The note read: 'Excuse me sir. Please kindly may I ask you a favour? May you meet me at this opened door?'

90

I spun around, hoping to find the town beauty framed in the doorway of one of the mud huts nearby. Instead I saw a young bleary-eyed guy swaying in a doorway and waving a brown beer bottle at me. I wandered over and found ten young, smelly men biting the tops off bottles and guzzling the contents of a powerful home brew called *Wanzuki*, made from the local honey. At 50 Tanzanian shillings a bottle (about 12 cents) it was a cheap way of forgetting that I was a nobody stuck in a nowhere town in the middle of a nowhere continent.

Will anyone try to get me drunk in order to take advantage of me?

If you're a girl, yes. In that way, travelling is not unlike going out at home.

If you're a guy—you wish!

What about the quality of the alcohol?

It depends on where you're travelling. For some beverages, you could be right at the source, sampling a Pilsner in its home town of Pilsen in the Czech Republic or drinking burgundy in, er, Burgundy, France.

You should note, however, that while it is undeniably cheaper to drink at the source, it is not necessarily a guarantee of quality. Chances are all that you're getting is the slops from the bottom of the barrel. All the good stuff has been sent off overseas to the lucrative export markets.

What about chemical additives?

Unable to grow hops—or cruelly robbed of the opportunity of buying any by unfortunate trade balances—many poorer countries turn to the wonders of modern chemistry to produce the natural malty flavour of their beers.

Of course, the distinctive taste of additives is immediately apparent, even to the least discerning of drinkers, so brewers compensate by upping the alcohol level to a point where after the first couple of sips drinkers are too plastered to notice or remember. In fact, the first you'll probably realise that you've been drinking a heavily processed beer is when you wake up the next morning with your hair on the pillow beside you. Safari Beer in Tanzania is particularly notorious for this.

What if I am a two-pot screamer?

Not a problem. In fact, it's better if you are. For one thing, you won't embarrass the locals by drinking them under the table—probably their only point of pride. They can leave you slumped over a couple of empties, content in the knowledge that while you might be able to travel around the world at will, visiting exotic locales and sampling different cultures, you can't hold your piss as well as they can.

91

Tell me about Happy Hours

A Happy Hour is a period of time—usually an hour or so—when the proprietor of a drinking establishment magnanimously agrees to make a slightly less obscene profit and sell drinks at half price. It is becoming more and more of a feature in the travel spots of the world, especially in Bali, Majorca and other haunts of those whose idea of a good holiday is getting totally rat-faced.

The actual name 'Happy Hour' has a fuzzy and unclear heritage, with many mistakenly believing that it refers to broad smiles on the punters' faces when they realise that they only have to shell out half their weekly wage on a round of drinks. In reality, it refers to the joyous state of the publican when he realises that he has got people drinking like fish at a time when staff are usually polishing glasses. What's more, they'll probably be too drunk to move on when he quadruples prices.

What's your advice on heavy nights before a long journey?

Just accept heavy nights as a fact of travelling life. It is inevitable that you will have a huge night of drunken debauchery the evening before you have to get up to catch a once-a-week bus at 5 am.

In your hung-over state you may be tempted to stay in bed and avoid facing the 16-hour bus journey. Don't. From my experience with the kind of places that only have a bus once a week, it is much, much worse to stay that week than endure a bus journey—no matter how crowded, long or horrific it promises to be.

Can I go on an alcohol-intensive tour?

Sure. Just jump on one of the countless 18–35 tours of Europe and you can drink yourself stupid in more countries, and in front of more well-known landmarks, than you could ever have imagined. You can do the same thing on half the backpacker tours operating in Australia.

You see, tour operators realised long ago what a potent mix travel, alcohol and sex starved young people is and the obscene amounts those people will pay for even the hint of getting laid.

Alcohol also has the added advantages of blurring the memory of the participants, cutting down on the number of complaints about the discrepancy between reality and the itinerary, and on law suits over the quality of the food.

No, I mean like the Oktoberfest

Oh. You're talking real specialist stuff aren't you?

I should admit at this stage that despite being Australian and despite having been to Germany a couple of times, I have never been to an Oktoberfest or a German beer hall for that matter. I have, however, extensively grilled someone who has—my very good friend Sean.

Sean made three points that any backpacker contemplating an Oktoberfest should take into account:

1. While large, the steins are filled with watered down beer.
2. While busty, the girls dextrously bearing the steins are also dextrous in any number of martial arts. What's more, they are unafraid of using these skills on any intoxicated lecher.
3. The band will play requests, but only if you buy them a beer. It is better, Sean suggests, to entice Americans to sing 'God Save the Queen' in exchange for lighting their cigarettes.

Finally, perhaps Sean's most sage piece of advice: avoid sitting near a table of Australians. They are likely to throw up on you.

TOP 10 BIG NIGHTS OUT

What is it that makes a big night out? Is it the company? Is it the setting? Or is it the copious amounts of alcohol consumed? In my experience it is the combination of all three. Below I have listed ten occasions when these mystical elements converged to create an unforgettable night out. God only knows about the bigger nights out that I can't even remember.

1.   Bwejuu Beach, Zanzibar, Tanzania

A sleepy collection of huts on the seldom-visited east coast of Zanzibar, Bwejuu Beach doesn't immediately strike you as one of the party capitals of the world. And after a week or so there it still doesn't. It's not until you turn to potent local Scotch in quiet desperation that things begin to pick up. Orange in colour and unrecognisable in taste, the Scotch has the ability to turn Bwejuu into a swinging place where the stars are more vibrant and the conversation witty and urbane. The mandatory two-month detox in the rather shabby Tanzanian equivalent of the Betty Ford Clinic is a bit of a worry though.

2.   Buzz Bar, Ölüdeniz, Turkey

Stuck on the rooftop of one of the restaurants lining the promenade of this tiny Turkish resort town, the Buzz Bar has no illusions about what it has been put on this earth to do. It's motto 'Go hard or go home' is emblazoned on signs along the windy mountain road into town and on the wall as you enter. I took the former option one balmy summer's night with a group of English film students and only the dexterity of a particularly alert waiter saved me from going home in a wooden box. The way he deftly plucked me from the edge of a 10-metre drop as I swayed atop a table trying to take a photo suggests I wasn't the first drunken yobbo he had rescued.

93

3.   The Night & Day Bar, Malindi, Kenya

What can you say about a place where the women bite off the tops of beer bottles and the fattest of them pins you against the back wall, grinding her generous pelvis into yours and slurring 'I don't want to fuck ya, I just want to welcome ya to Kenya'? Well, if you're my friend Sean, not much at all. He wandered into the Night & Day Bar one fateful New Year's Eve four years ago and he's never quite recovered.

4.   The Church, London, England

Mindless drinking games, wet T-shirt and wet jock competitions, crude, unfunny comedians and a soundtrack of songs whose only distinguishing feature is a moronic chorus that the yobbos can sing along to—this, my friends, is what passes for Australian culture in London. Held every Sunday in a warehouse with sawdust on the floor and plastic bins full of ice and six packs of VB at the back, the Church is often the subject of sensational exposés by the British media who take great delight in showing young Antipodeans drinking themselves into a stupor and falling stylelessly into their own vomit. The venue is always changing, supposedly to avoid licensing laws, but in reality it is to protect the organisers from a team of deadly assassins hired by the Australia Council.

94

5.   The Fairy Chimneys, Göreme, Turkey

After a night on the raki in a cafe where a guy sat in the corner playing a strange stringed instrument in a most discordant and unpleasant manner, a group of us got the great idea of spending the night in one of the eerie troglodyte dwellings that surround the town. The dwellings had been carved into the strange finger-like formations by Cappadocians centuries before, so we clambered up into one of the most isolated, lit a fire, put on some tapes and continued with the raki. Our plan to watch the sun rise over the weird moonscape environment was rudely scarpered when we were raided just after midnight by the Turkish army and detained on suspicion of being PKK terrorists.

6. Queen's Cafe, Hanoi, Vietnam

There's nothing special about the Queen's Cafe in the old part of Hanoi. It's just another cramped and sweaty restaurant packed with travellers who have just returned from a tour to Sapa or Halong Bay wearing their complimentary Queen's Cafe T-shirts. But the Chinese beer is cold and cheap and the alcohol content ambiguous, making it the perfect place to start a big night out—so good a place, in fact, that it is the only thing I remember from my last night in Hanoi. That, and waking up the next morning in the Polite Bar on the other side of town.

95

7. Various Irish Bars, Madrid

As soon as I fell in with a bunch of 'hens' from Wigan on a pub crawl around Sol (Madrid's raucous bar district) this evening was never going to end prettily. Letting them talk me into drinking pints of Red Bull and Vodka only made the inevitable happen sooner. Now, somewhere in northern England there are some incriminating photos of me with a (male) blow-up doll. And in a small hotel on the Calle Victoria there is a proprietor who has vowed never to let an Aussie near his bidets again.

8. The world's smallest sukiyaki restaurant, Shibuya, Japan

I find that sake is one of those drinks that kind of sneaks up on you. It's fine as long as you remain seated, but as soon as you stand up you're in all kinds of trouble. Like on this night, for example. I was eating in the upstairs cupboard of a restaurant so pushed for space that meals were sent up on a trolley in a dumb waiter. Well into evening I decided to go to the toilet—in effect the laneway out the back—and attempted to clamber down the staircase. I took one step and before I knew it my heels were ricocheting along the rungs making a sound not unlike that of a stick being run along a chain wire fence. Incredibly I landed on my feet, amidst a group of startled Japanese diners. With a florid hand-movement, I went 'Da-Daa!', and received a polite round of applause.

9. Florida 2000, Nairobi, Kenya

We didn't know it at the time, but the Florida 2000 is one of those places established for the express intent of introducing economically-disadvantaged African girls to economically-advantaged Westerners. The fact that we were taken there by a lecherous Queenslander who claimed to be able to distinguish the village of origin of African girls by the way they groomed their pubic hair should have set the alarm bells ringing. But it didn't, so we spent the first part of the evening fending off the advances of some rather predatory women. (One of whom, a Ugandan, pulled my head back by the hair and whispered huskily 'I want you. Now!') They soon gave up, however, when they realised that in true Aussie fashion we weren't buying them drinks. They turned their attentions instead to two Germans in safari suits and we had a wonderful night watching them dance with true Teutonic grace.

10. Numerous bars and dens of iniquity, Prague, Czech Republic

It was my last night in Prague and I was all alone. Feeling sorry for myself, I wandered into a nearby *pivnice* with the intent of eating and going back to the empty hostel to mope. Thankfully, a nearby table of young soldiers spotted me and turned what was looking like a miserable night into one of my best nights in the Czech Republic. They were on leave until 7 o'clock the next morning and were determined to go back smashed. What's more, they were determined that I was going to go down with them. It was such a good night, staggering from one smoky Czech bar to another, that I very nearly enlisted myself.

96

Chapter 11

VISAS

Visas—you can't live with them, and a lot of countries can't live without the extra cash they bring in. Here's the dirt on the bane of most travellers' lives.

What is a visa and why do I have to spend good money getting one?

The official story is that a visa is a stamp placed in your passport by a foreign country allowing you to visit for a certain amount of time and for a certain purpose. In reality it is a thinly veiled excuse to milk you of hard-earned cash. While the amount varies and is rarely substantial, it is still usually enough for you to live on for a couple of days.

97

What determines the cost of a visa?

As a general rule, the less appealing the country, the less endowed with natural and man-made wonders, the more the visa will cost you. Similarly, the cost of a visa will be totally disproportionate to the amount of time you plan to spend in the country. The country you plan to spend the least amount of time in will invariably have the most expensive visa. A friend of mine, for example, had to spend A $48 for a visa to spend 48 hours in Pakistan. As he is fond of telling anyone who cares to listen, that works out at $1 an hour.

When can I expect a visa to be expensive?

You can expect a visa to cost a bomb when:

o   It's a poor shithole of a country that no one in their right mind would want to visit.

o   You have never heard of the country.

- They insist on being paid in US dollars or German marks.
- The country has a Socialist, Marxist or Communist regime.
- You are only in transit.
- The country is smack bang in the middle of two countries you want to visit and can't afford to fly between.
- Your country just expelled two of their diplomats for drug smuggling, paedophilia or nuclear arms procurement.
- Your Prime Minister just called their Prime Minister a recalcitrant.

Is there anything endearing about visas?

Not surprisingly, a lot of people hate visas. Call me contrary, but I love them. Sure they cost a lot of money, but there is something strangely satisfying about pulling out your passport after a long journey and flicking through them. They're like a journal—little graphic reminders of where you have been and what it was like. Each smudge, each florid signature, each iconoclastic emblem has a story to tell.

Are visas a badge of honour?

In some circles, wankier circles to be sure, visas *are* considered a badge of honour. It sounds pathetic, but at any given time you will come across groups of grown people showing off stamps that are no more sophisticated than the ones they used to get in primary school. Even more disturbing is the fact that they are getting off on the ritual. It is a scene being played out in bars, restaurants, cafes and hostels around the world even as we speak.

These sessions, usually induced by overconsumption of a local brew, will illicit the full gamut of human emotions. *Pride* at having an Egyptian visa that incorporates three postage stamps instead of the usual one. *Shame* at only having a Malaysian visa and the joke visa given out at Sea World on the Gold Coast. *Jealousy* at the bastard with the rare Somalian visa from the Siyad Barre era. And finally, *deflation* at learning that, like everything else in life, there is always someone with a bigger, brighter and more bizarre one than you.

98

All my visas are boring. Is there anything I can do about it?

Sometimes it may be worthwhile getting an obscure visa, say for Afghanistan or Angola, even if you have no intention of going there. As a general rule, by the time fellow travellers are flicking through your passport they will be fairly inebriated. They'll notice the visa, but won't go searching for the smaller, less spectacular entry and exit visas that actually prove that you've visited the country. The upshot of this is that because you have the visa, the inference will be made that you have visited the country, thus earning you brownie points as a guru traveller.

99

If you plan to play along with this misconception it may be wise to avoid any question about the country you were supposed to have visited. If questioned, just shrug your shoulders. If really pushed, indicate that it was such an ordeal that you would rather not talk about it. Any visible scar that you may have should be absent-mindedly rubbed at this point.

Is it true that visas are the mirror of a country's soul?

I've always found that you can tell a lot about a country from its visa. Take Singapore, for example. Its visa is small, neat and practical—a bit like Singapore itself. Visas for African countries, like Zaire, are often huge and grandiose, but are stamped in ink that fades overnight. Australian and American visas, on the other hand, are dour and soulless. They look like they have been designed by a committee of politically correct public servants.

What about the way a visa is stamped?

This, too, can tell you a lot about a country. Take our good friends the Singaporeans again. They will diligently search through your passport to find the most convenient place to stamp it—usually a space amongst other visas that you despaired of ever using. If, after searching through your passport for a couple of days, the Singaporeans can't find such a space, they will ask your permission before stamping a fresh page. It should come as no surprise to you then that in Singapore you can be fined S$500 for not flushing the toilet.

Indonesians, on the other hand, have a habit of sticking their visas any old place they feel like—usually on the first page that falls open—and hence can't be used for anything else but a Singaporean visa. Anyone who has ever caught a bus in Indonesia will tell you that, once again, this is an accurate reflection of the national spirit.

Should I get all my visas before I go?

100

There is a school of thought that you should sort out all your visa requirements in your own country before you start travelling. There are even companies who, for a small fee, will organise your visas for you. All you have to do is fill in the forms and supply three passport-size photos. This is of course an eminently sensible idea. All the guidebooks suggest that you do it this way. Your mother would suggest you do it this way. All I can say is, whatever you do, don't do it. You will be robbing yourself of one of travel's most enriching and enjoyable experiences—the 'Great Visa Chase'.

What is the Great Visa Chase?

The Great Visa Chase is where you spend an inordinate amount of time and money traipsing around a foreign city trying to line up a visa for the next country on your itinerary—sometimes, unkindly, referred to as the 'wild goose chase'.

What's in the Great Visa Chase for me?

A lot actually. You get to see a part of a foreign city that you usually wouldn't have seen. You get to travel on transport that you shouldn't have been on. And, most importantly, you get a visa that you wouldn't have, or shouldn't have, otherwise got.

Take an Iranian visa, for example. You could apply for one before you leave, but the Iranians might well insist on something like a personal letter of recommendation from the Ayatollah (the dead one) and a public rendition of your favourite verse from the Koran. Then, after six months, they'll refuse to give you one anyway. If you apply in a neighbouring country like Turkey, Syria or Pakistan, they'll only insist on the letter.

TOP 10
FAVOURITE
EMBASSIES

As an aficionado of the Great Visa Chase, I have spent more than my fair share of time traipsing around the backblocks of forgotten cities searching for hidden embassies and chasing elusive visas. As such, I thought I'd share with you the names of some of the embassies that have brought me the greatest joy over the years.

1. Vietnamese Embassy, New Dehli

Even if you have no intention of going to Vietnam, it's always fun having these guys refuse to give you a visa. Ask to see the Cultural Attaché. He still thinks there's a war on.

2. São Tomé Embassy, Libreville

Attached precariously to a disintegrating concrete house in the 'African' part of Libreville, this embassy has seen better days. But if you arrive at mealtime you'll have the opportunity to sample traditional West African fare. The Ambassador's mother cooks it on the floor over a charcoal fire, just in front of the visa desk.

3. US Embassy, Libreville

The library is a great place to sit out the not-so-infrequent riots. At the slightest hint of trouble, all the doors and windows are automatically sealed by metal bars—a lot like the closing credits of *Get Smart*.

4. Albanian Embassy, Budapest

See how far you can get into the embassy before anyone challenges your right to be there. I got as far as the Ambassador's bedroom before being busted by the maid making his bed. The grounds are also popular with mating Hungarian couples.

101

5. Somalian Embassy, Nairobi

Not so much the embassy itself, but the thrill of finding where it is this week. I visited International House, the Jacaranda Hotel and a local brothel before finding it in a nondescript townhouse on the edge of town. God only knows where it is now.

6. Australian Embassy, Nairobi

Perhaps the purest expression of the true purpose of an Australian embassy. Always—and only—filled with backpackers, it's a great place to swap information. Ask for the visitor's book. It's the most reliable way to find accommodation in Nairobi with hot water.

7. Australian Embassy, Islamabad

Specifically, 'The Coolibah Club'. On Thursday nights it's one of the few places in this strict Muslim town where you'll be able to buy a beer. If his football team won that week, the High Commissioner might even let you swim in the pool.

8. Afghanistan Consulate, Peshawar

Only open Mondays and Thursdays, but still packs a wallop. Mingle with international drug dealers and arms merchants and fight over the spot on the couch with gun-toting mujaheddin.

9. German Embassy, London

Or any of the embassies bordering Hyde Park. A great way to see how the other half live and reconfirm that Britain really is a class-conscious society.

10. Sudanese Embassy, Addis Ababa

Run by a guy with hair like Einstein and the attitude of the Soup Nazi from *Seinfeld*, if you don't follow instructions to the letter you'll be yelled at, kicked out and told to come back the next day. Disturbingly, it's the easiest place to get a Sudanese visa in Africa.

Chapter 12

PLANES

What a wondrous thing the aeroplane is—a magical lump of metal that can transport you halfway across the world and back in less than a day. In one fell swoop it has defeated the tyranny of distance, opening up new corners of the world to be despoiled by undiscerning backpackers. However, in doing so it has introduced new tyrannies to be conquered— pallid airline food, airport taxi drivers and the most monstrous of all, the middle-aged, frumpy flight attendant who seems to have real problems with backpackers and their natural urge to drink as much free booze and eat as many complimentary peanuts as possible.

Is flying philosophically kosher?

In your travels you will come across sad individuals who refuse to fly because it supposedly divorces them from the pure travelling experience. As far as these folk are concerned, flying is easy, free of the hardships and the uncertainties that constitute *real* travelling. Supposedly, the modern traveller just turns up at the airport, boards a well-maintained aircraft and spends the few hours being showered with cordon bleu meals and complimentary single-malt whisky.

Anyone who has bought a ticket from a dodgy bucket shop knows that this just isn't true. For one thing, the simple act of checking in is as arduous as any Himalayan trek and demands just as much preparation. And that's not even taking into account the dubious safety records of many of the aircraft involved. I'm pleased to say that these flights are equally as gruelling, vague and life-threatening as any 'real' journey into the heart of Africa or LA.

103

Some absolute inevitabilities of flying

Many people consider flying a thing of mystery and intrigue, a magical experience where anything and everything will occur. Not true. There are some realities you can count on *always* happening.

104

For example:

o   The air-conditioning will break down in the airport where you have to spend eight hours waiting for a connecting flight.

o   You will have seen all the movies showing on the plane. And if you haven't seen them, there's a very good reason why.

o   The food cart will run out of food just as it reaches your row and then it will take another half an hour to get reloaded and come back.

o   The food cart will arrive while you are at the toilet, blocking the path back to your seat.

o   The toilet will be occupied when you really need to go.

o   The only good-looking flight attendant will be serving on the opposite side of the plane to you.

o   You will be seated next to the fattest, craziest, smelliest or most psychotic person on the plane. If it is a long flight, they will suffer from a combination of all four disorders.

o   The plane will hit a particularly rough patch of turbulence just as the flight attendant is attempting to pour your coffee.

How safe is flying?

We've all heard the hoary old chestnut that it is safer to fly than drive, but just how true is it?

It all depends on the age and condition of the plane you're flying in. A new plane stands a better chance of staying in the air, even if it's only because the odds are in its favour. And, of course, it depends on luck. After all, the CAAC pilots don't mistakenly lock themselves out of the cockpit *every* day.

How can I tell the age of an aeroplane?

You can get a rough idea of the age of a plane by looking at it. But if you really want to get an accurate answer you have to look inside it. Thankfully, the telltale signs should be well within reach from the comfort—or otherwise—of your seat.

First, look at the buckle on your seat belt. Does the embossed airline logo match the name of the airline on your ticket? If it does, congratulations. You are flying what I call a 'first generation' aircraft—a plane that has come straight from the factory to the airline in question. Everything should be in relatively good working order.

If the logos don't match, don't be overly concerned. You are probably flying on a 'second generation' aircraft—a plane bought second-hand from one of the major airlines by a carrier not quite able to raise the cash for a new one. Like I said, nothing to worry about. A lot of the major airlines change their planes every two years, so the aircraft involved may still be a relative youngster. And with the strict maintenance standards of many of the major players you may well want to regard the aircraft as 'pre-loved'.

Of course, that's not to say that the plane isn't even older. To find out if your aircraft is third, fourth or even multi-generational, look for these other clues:

o The airline logo in the bottom right-hand corner of the safety card in the seat pocket in front of you has been crossed out and replaced a number of times.

o The airsickness bag has had just as many changes in logos and is yellow and cracked with age.

o None of the logos on the cutlery that comes with your meal match.

o And then there's the real give away—paint peeling off the tail to reveal an old PanAm logo.

105

Should I shop around for an airfare?

An airfare is the most important investment you'll make as a traveller—more expensive than the combined bar bill of your entire journey and more costly than the carpet you didn't really want but ended up buying anyway at the Grand Bazaar in Istanbul.

As such, buying an airfare should be treated with the same diligence as buying your first home. Scour the newspapers for

106

cheap flights; harass travel agents into giving you the cheapest airfare and not just the one that gives them the most obscene commission; and finally, book as far in advance as possible. Having done all that, realise that the day after you pay for your flight you'll find a significantly cheaper one. Or at best, the bucket shop will go bust and mysteriously disappear with all your money.

What about these no-frills airlines? Are they good value?

Over the years the airline industry has seen a number of no-frills operators come and go. In the eighties it was Peoples Airline, flying between London and North America. A more recent example is the 'peanuts and coke' flights between Australia and New Zealand.

No-frills airlines work on the general premise of cutting back on the accoutrements like free booze and inedible food, and passing the savings onto the consumer. What you've got to decide is how much you *really* save. Subtract the cost of the cheap ticket from that of a normal one to discover the difference. Then decide whether you'll drink the equivalent, or more, in alcohol. I'm yet to meet a backpacker who has tackled this equation and still taken the cheaper flight.

Everything you wanted to know about airports but were afraid to ask

o   They are always at least 50 kilometres, two hours or an outrageous taxi fare away from all the cheap hotels and hostels.

o   Inexpensive local buses into the city centre always stop running 10 minutes before the arrival of cheap flights. Similarly, they don't start running again until 10 minutes after the cheap flights depart.

o   Airport seats are specifically designed to be impossible to sleep on.

o   Security guards, cleaners and other airport employees will sometimes let you sleep on the floor at an airport if your flight arrives late or leaves early. Once you are comfortable— or the last bus or taxi has departed—their shift will end and the people replacing them will kick you out of the terminal.

o   Airport food is even worse than airline food. Worse still, you have to pay for it and pay dearly.

o   With the exception of Singapore's Changi Airport and possibly the new airport just off Osaka, airports are architecturally uninspiring and designed to trigger even the most repressed psychosis.

o   The words 'duty free' mean something totally different at airports. Throw in a whiff of avgas and it becomes normal recommended retail price—then some!

o   Airport banks work to office hours, even though planes don't.

o   There are always more immigration counters than there are immigration officers.

o   There are always more passengers than immigration forms.

o   There are always more check-in counters than check-in staff.

Is a window seat the best seat on the plane?

A lot of people plump for a window seat under the mistaken assumption that they are actually going to see something. But unless you get off on watching clouds for hours on end—and I know that some of you do, especially if you've taken some of those funny air sickness tablets—you won't actually see much of interest. In fact, the only time you're likely to see anything is during take off and landing and if you're anything like me, you will have your eyes firmly closed at that moment anyway. You should also note that coming into some airports, like Hong Kong's Kai Tak for example, the captain will actively encourage passengers to pull down the little plastic shutters to prevent mass panic.

Another problem with window seats becomes apparent the moment you want to go to the toilet. It seems to be **107** airline policy to seat the most obese people on the plane in the two seats between a window seat and the aisle, effectively blocking your path to the nearest convenience. I'm sure it has something to do with distributing weight equally over the aircraft, but I have a sneaking suspicion that it could also be the by-product of malicious check-in attendants, sick of every second person asking them for a window seat.

108

What about aisle seats then?

In theory, aisle seats are great. You're not hemmed in by the plane's token Jenny Craig drop-out and you have the added benefit of being able to stretch your legs in the passageway. The reality is that if you did stretch your legs there's every likelihood that you'd have them amputated by the constantly patrolling food and duty free trolleys. And when they're not about, there are the drunks roaming the aisles looking for somewhere to throw up. Chances are they'll trip and land in your lap, often with dire consequences.

Well, where's the best seat then?

As a general rule, anywhere other than the seat you are allocated. It also depends on who you're flying with. If you're bound for Cali in Colombia with American Airlines, I'd have to say the one closest to the exit.

How can I avoid jet lag?

Avoid jets.

What can I do to make my flight more comfortable?

You may be surprised to learn that clothing— or more precisely, lack of it—plays an important role in making your flight a less traumatic experience.

You see, when you fly, your whole body swells up—something to do with the fact that flying is an unnatural act and that if God had meant us to fly he would have given us all wings or, at the very least, a frequent flyer card. Therefore it is a good idea to fly naked or if that is impractical, wear loose-fitting clothes. That way you can accommodate all the changes your body will undergo throughout the flight. It sounds like puberty all over again, doesn't it?

Should I take my shoes off?

Nowhere is this swelling more severe than in your extremities and, in particular, your feet. But should you decide to remove your shoes, make sure you take two issues into consideration: one, you may not be able to put your shoes back on at the end of the flight; and two, unless you have just changed your Odour Eaters, you may be unpopular with the other passengers around you.

What about joining the mile-high club?

Sex, sex, sex. That's all you ever think about, isn't it? Well, I'm not going to titillate your sordid mind with tales of cockpit copulation here. You'll find that sort of thing in the chapter entitled 'Sex and Romance'.

Some other fun things to do while flying

The most dangerous thing about flying is the amount of time it gives you to think. Once the meals have been served, the movies watched and the loop of turgid tunes listened to, there isn't much else to do other than ponder upon what a mess you're making of your life.

Coming from Australia, where the nearest land mass of any significance is over eight hours away (I apologise in advance to any of my Kiwi readers), it is a problem I've had to face every time I've left the country. In order to avoid subjecting my innermost feelings to that kind of unrelenting exposure, I've come up with the following activities guaranteed to keep soul-searching at bay:

109

o   Grip the handles of your seat, squeeze your eyes tight and groan, 'We're all going to die, we're all going to die'.

o   Push the button that summons the flight attendant on the console of the seat next to you while the person beside you isn't looking. Repeat until the flight attendant loses his or her temper and reports the person next to you to the captain for harassment.

o   Change the sound channel on the con-
    sole of the person next to you just
    at the climax of the movie.
    Then apologise profusely,
    claiming that you thought it
    was yours.

o   Adjust your seat forwards
    and then backwards as
    the person behind you is
    trying to eat their meal.

o   Attempt to break David
    Boon's record for the most
    number of beers drunk on a
    flight from Sydney to London,
    or at least tell everyone around
    you, very loudly, that you are going to
    try.

110

(For all you philistines out there, David Boon—or 'Stumpy' as he is
affectionately known—batted at number three for the Australian
cricket team and was an excellent close-in fieldsman.)

TOP 10 NIGHTMARE FLIGHTS

What is it that makes a bad flight bad? Well, crashing is obviously not a good thing nor is an emergency landing or a hijack situation. Unfortunately, such occurrences are rare and it is rather more mundane things these days that make a poor flight. Like a surly flight attendant, a patch of turbulence, a boring movie or something like the following 10 incidents.

1. Rangoon to Bangkok, Burma Air

When I first tried to get on this flight I was told it was full. I should have immediately sussed then that something was amiss when a few minutes later some seats miraculously appeared—for fifteen of us!

Aboard the Fokker it soon became apparent how this miracle occurred. Burma Air had simply bolted in a few extra rows of seats, each with broken fold-down tables covered in graffiti. As we taxied onto the runway, our knees under our chins, the unsmiling flight attendant kicked broken armrests under our seats and tossed us a cardboard box with a complimentary sandwich. As we took off, swarms of tiny German cockroaches crawled from between the window and made a jump for the runway. I was tempted to join them.

2. Cairo to Athens, Olympic Airways

Halfway through this flight the plane dipped sharply 90 degrees to the right and then 180 degrees just as sharply to the left. The incident probably would have gone relatively unnoticed except for the fact that the flight attendant abandoned the food trolley and ran screaming to the cockpit to see what had happened. I spent the rest of the flight clutching the armrests, realising just how much blind faith in your pilot contributes to a sound and peaceful flight.

111

3. Mt Newman to Port Hedland, Western Australia, BHP private plane

When you spend an hour or so in a small single-engined Cessna you realise why they invented 747s with reclining seats, in-flight entertainment and flight attendants to cater for your every whim—and also why the air sickness bag was invented.

4. Karachi to Nairobi, Pakistan International Airways

To be honest, this flight wasn't too bad. I was just left a little unsettled by the captain's insistence on ending each of his messages with *inshallah*—Arabic for 'God willing'. In the course of the flight we were going to cruise at an altitude of 33,000 feet—God willing—cross over the horn of Africa—God willing—and finally land at Nairobi Airport—God willing. Even the in-flight movie was presented to us subject to divine wishes. If that wasn't enough, the sight of the entire planeload of passengers lying prostrate in the aisles at prayer time really pushed me over the edge. I spent the rest of the flight mumbling *inshallah* myself.

5. Kigali to Bujumbura, Rwanda Air

We left Kigali in torrential rains and arrived in Bujumbura as they were evacuating all the foreigners in a big Air France jumbo because of a massacre going on in downtown Bujumbura. Yes, I guess you could say that it was an interesting flight.

6. Sydney to Athens, Olympic Airways

When it comes to in-flight service, you can't go past the smiling, friendly ways of Greece's national carrier. As soon as the safety demonstrations are over and the plane is up in the air, the lovely ladies of Olympic barricade themselves in the galley for a fag and a chinwag, never to be seen again for the rest of the flight.

And God help anyone who disturbs them. The lady sitting next to me on this particular flight had a headache and after unsuccessfully buzzing the flight attendant for three hours bravely decided to go up to the galley and ask for an aspirin. She came back empty handed and chastened by a surly flight attendant who, after hearing her request, snapped 'What do you think we are? A bloody chemist?'

113

7.   London to Brisbane, Qantas

The portents for this flight weren't good. I was rushing home to see my sister who was in intensive care with pneumonia. I got trapped against the window by a mother and her screaming child. I could have coped with that—I had my Walkman—except that the Qantas flight attendant insisted I move to a seat in the centre aisle. I had barely settled in when I was asked to move again, this time for a little old lady with gout. Half an hour later I moved again. The flight crew had obviously figured that it was better to inconvenience one passenger four times than four passengers once each. I spent the entire 22 hours as the token put-upon passenger.

8.   Lagos to Rio, Varig

After checking my bag and issuing me with a boarding card, the good folk of Varig then decided not to allow me on board without a Brazilian visa, even though a few days before they assured me that I didn't need one. After a frantic taxi ride back into Lagos and a humiliating scene where I prostrated myself before the Brazilian Consul and begged him for a stamp, I was finally let on board seconds before the once-a-week flight took off.

There is a happy ending though. By that stage, economy was full, so I ended up being upgraded to business class where I enjoyed rump steak served on proper crockery and chatted with the guy next to me about the rare stumpy-legged goat he had smuggled on board in the hold.

9.   Leticia to Bogotá, Satena

Run by the Colombian military, Satena services the parts of Colombia no one else will—like Leticia, deep in the Amazon bordering Peru and Brazil. The fact that the jungle surrounding Leticia is riddled with laboratories producing cocaine meant that I spent the entire flight in the company of some very dubious characters, including some goldfish in plastic drums with very erratic swimming habits.

10.   Lisala to Mbandaka, Scibe-Airlift

It was my original intention to catch this little ten-seater all the way down to Mbandaka. But when the right-hand engine caught fire as we prepared to take off from Lisala, I decided to bail out while I still could. I made my way down to the Zaire River to catch a barge instead, leaving two guys with buckets of sand to try and put the fire out.

114

Chapter 13

TRAINS

To many people rail travel is an ageing technology—a rusting, creaking dinosaur from an era when iron and coal ruled the roost and the sun never set on the British Empire.

It's true. And in those far-flung corners of the Empire, you'll still find trains and stations and railway lines that haven't been touched since their colonial creators left.

115

But if the truth be known, that's the charm of travelling by train. With a little imagination one can be transported to a time when the world was still mysterious and untamed and air-conditioned comfort was unheard of—and to a place where mankind eats, drinks, shits and screws right before your very eyes.

Where does the term the 'romance of rail' come from?

Contrary to popular opinion, it is not the opulence of trains like the Orient Express that gives rail travel the air of romance, nor is it the echoes of past glories one often finds in the ageing steam trains of India.

It is rather more simple and sordid than that. Compared to other modes of travelling like planes and buses, it is quite feasible to indulge in a little horizontal folk dancing on a train without getting arrested or doing yourself an injury.

What are the benefits of travelling by train?

More celibate readers will be pleased to know that there are other, more beneficial reasons for travelling by train than just indulging in a little 'romance'. They include:

Safety

Let's be frank here. A plane falls out of the sky and your chances of surviving are negligible. If you're on a train that crashes, however, chances are you'll get off with a few scratches and bruises and maybe the embarrassment of having your face in the lap of the guy sitting opposite you.

Of course, that equation changes if you're on an Indian train. A particularly rough shunting there and half the passengers seem to cark it.

Scenery

Unlike planes, when you travel on a train you actually get to see something other than clouds and the head of the person in front of you. And unlike buses, it is usually more picturesque and interesting than the roadhouse on a multi-lane freeway.

It's not all rolling fields and flowers, though. I am yet to approach a major city by train without witnessing some of the most appalling scenes of poverty and squalor. Melbourne is particularly bad for this.

Company

People seem to be more relaxed and friendly on trains, and more likely to strike up a conversation. But if they begin to bore you, you can get up and go for a stroll. By the time you come back they're either talking to someone else, have fallen asleep or gotten off, taking all your luggage with them.

Leg room

For anyone over 4'9" (145 cm for the young and imperically challenged) who is used to travelling on buses and planes with their knees under their chin, trains are a major revelation. Even the discomfort of having domestic animals and undomesticated children tethered to your seat cannot detract from the luxury of space that rail travel usually offers.

116

Cost

Nine times out of ten, rail travel is a fraction of the cost of air travel. The exceptions are countries like China and Vietnam where authorities see the humble rail journey as another fantastic opportunity to separate backpackers from their money.

Is rail travel *really* cheaper?

117

If you were to do a straight out comparison between the cost of an air ticket and that of a train ticket, a train ticket is going to win out every time. But you're right. There's more to the cost of a train ticket than the cash you hand over to a disinterested ticket seller.

Firstly, there's the matter of time. A rail journey, on average, is going to take ten to twenty times longer than flying, considerably more if you're in Africa or India. Now if you're a backpacker that doesn't matter much. Your time isn't worth anything anyway. But for everyone else, it's something to take into consideration.

Secondly, there's the question of comfort. Conventional wisdom has it that a train is more comfortable than a plane because you can get up and walk around. But what about the times when you will be wedged in so tight that you can't go for a walk even if you wanted to? Or the fact that if you did, someone would nick your seat and force you to spend the rest of the journey standing?

Thirdly, there's the torturous design of train seats to take into account. Employing what I like to call 'disergonomics', the average train seat is comfortable to sit in for ten minutes maximum. Beyond that, they appear to be specifically designed to cramp muscles and jar bones that you didn't even know you had.

And finally, rail travel is not always cheaper. Kilometre for kilometre, the London Underground is actually more expensive than flying. I don't know where I got that bit of information, but it's the perfect lead into the next question—the vexing question of underground railways.

The vexing question of underground railways

These days, the urban centres of most big cities have some sort of rail system. Even Los Angeles, long the hold-out against cheap, clean public transport, has recently splashed out on an inner city light rail system.

Some underground railways are modern and efficient like the Singapore MTR. There the train is hermetically sealed from the platform by a glass wall and doors that open only when the train has safely come to a halt to prevent suicides. Others are more decrepit, like the one in Budapest, built in the late 1800s, never serviced since and too slow to do any damage to even the most determined of jumpers. Regardless of their condition, most underground railway systems are a cheap and efficient way around their respective bustling metropolises.

The major exception is the London Underground. Not only is it expensive, it is also a confusing Byzantine maze that will see you spending so much time walking along tunnels that it is often quicker to surface and walk.

Are there any other problems with underground railways?

Apart from old wooden escalators catching fire, there are other less apparent drawbacks to using underground rail systems extensively. In particular, your whole impression of a city—and your orientation within it—could be totally determined by that city's underground railway system. There is a real danger that you'll emerge blinking from the station nearest the airport without having seen anything of the city above ground.

Don't laugh! I've met many travellers whose major impression of Piccadilly Circus is that it is where the Piccadilly line meets the Bakerloo line. Similarly, they don't remember Moszkva tér in Budapest as a bustling area full of bars and restaurants but rather as the station with the blue seats and the brushed aluminium siding.

Intra and international rail travel. The NSITT guide to class

It's when you decide to catch a train for longer distances that rail travel gets really interesting. Stroll up to a ticket office in any railway station anywhere in the world and you'll be confronted by a bewildering

118

array of tickets and options—first class, hard sleeper, hanging from the roof—all with an equally bewildering range of costs.

To help you with this decision—and let's face it, it could mean the difference between a truly great and a truly awful holiday—I've put this easy-to-use guide together.

119

Third class

Obscenely inexpensive and unfathomably uncomfortable, third class is where you are just as likely to be sharing your seat with a goat as a granny, and a whole herd at that. And don't expect any special treatment as a tourist. Most of these people have spent the equivalent of a couple of years salary on these tickets and they ain't moving for nobody. Having said that, you'll be surprised by the generosity of your fellow passengers in this class. They'll be constantly offering you food, if only to enjoy watching you screw your nose up at it.

Second class

Perhaps the best value option in Third World rail travel. More room to roam and a little less livestock, second class is the domain of those who want a little more comfort without losing the experience of Third World rail travel. The toilets still stink, and the seats are still uncomfortable, but at least you can go for a stroll without having to pick you way through an entire village camped out on the floor.

First class

The pinnacle of luxury on most rail services. What you must remember, however, is that first class does not necessarily mean carpet on the floor and chandeliers hanging from the ceiling. It is simply the very best that that particular train has to offer. Anyone who has seen the state of the trains in Africa and Asia knows that equates to not very much. In fact, I spent a few extra Egyptian pounds once to travel first class from Cairo to Aswan. The only discernible difference I could see between first and second class was that underneath all the shit on the floor in the first class toilet there was linoleum. In second class it was bare concrete.

What is a rail pass?

A rail pass is a piece of paper that costs a lot of money and allows you to rush around a continent without seeing anything, meeting anyone or ever relaxing.

How does it work?

It's quite a simple concept actually. Your rail pass will be valid for a certain period of time—either one month, two months or something more bizarre and incomprehensible like six and a half days. It will allow you to travel on any train within a certain group of countries within that period of time, except the most convenient, comfortable and quickest trains. You will be asked to pay a supplement for these services, the amount usually not being more than two or three times the price you originally paid for your pass.

What about these new-fangled passes?

Recently, the folk responsible for Eurail passes released an array of new passes that allow you to stagger the days you travel, allowing you to stay in a place that takes your fancy rather than rush off on the next train out for fear of not getting the best value from your pass.

120

On first glance, they appear to be just what the doctor ordered. But be wary. They come with all manner of rules and conditions that even the most devious of lawyers would be hard-pressed to understand.

Can I save money using rail passes?

Well, that's certainly the idea behind it. The cost of the rail pass should, in effect, be considerably cheaper than the sum of the cost of all the individual journeys you used it for.

If you're prepared to rush from one city to another, checking your baggage in the cloak room in the morning and catching an overnighter out again that evening, you'll find yourself getting extraordinary value out of your pass.

Are there any drawbacks to rail passes?

The major drawback I've found is this obsession with getting the most 'value' out of a rail pass.

A friend of mine was travelling around England on a Britrail pass when he met an attractive, intelligent Australian girl heading back to London. She was going to stay in her uncle's mansion in North London and invited him to stay with her for a week of cost-free romance. He still had five days left on his pass, so he declined. Rail passes tend to do that to you.

How can I cure my rail pass obsession?

It's quite simple. Look up the cost of the longest, most expensive rail journey you can do on your chosen pass. Once you are assured that it costs the same as your pass, or even a little less, make sure it is the first trip you do on your pass.

It may take one or two days out of your itinerary, but at least you'll enjoy the rest of your trip at a more leisurely pace assured in the knowledge that you've got your money's worth.

If you're one of those people who isn't happy unless you've really screwed the system, just spend the whole of your pass doing that trip over and over again.

Can trains save on accommodation?

Pick your trains right and you may never have to pay for a single night's accommodation. Simply catch overnight trains everywhere.

121

While this is quite feasible in the vast continents of Asia and the Americas, it's problematical in Europe. Most European countries are only an hour or so apart, meaning that you'll end up spending a lot of nights sleeping on railway station floors.

Is railway food edible?

Is the pope a Hindu? In western countries you'll find it bland and expensive. In the Third World it is cheap and alarming. (It's alarming in that you don't know exactly what it is you're getting, what it will taste like or whether it will kill you.)

Should I be wary of strangers offering me food?

In some countries it is not unknown for people of ill repute to offer travellers drugged tea or chocolates. Those who accept the offer often wake up hours later with all their valuables and even a major organ missing.

It's probably best then to politely refuse food from strangers. And with the state of the goods offered by passing railway food waiters, it's probably best if you regard them as strangers too.

What about security?

Unlike planes, where there isn't anywhere for a would-be thief to hide, trains offer the petty criminal ample opportunity to pilfer your belongings and escape unnoticed.

Once, when I travelled from Bangkok to Singapore by rail, the whole train was ransacked by gangs of thieves as we waited outside a small office on the Thai–Malaysian border to collect our freshly stamped passports. The train was then delayed even further as all those people silly enough to leave their cameras on their seat filed reports with the police.

In short, every time the train stops is an opportunity for you to lose everything you own and cherish. So keep your valuables close to you, chain your pack to the luggage rack and stay awake all night watching it. Then if you're lucky—very lucky—you might get to your destination with everything you started with. Except your sanity, of course.

122

TOP 10
UNFORGETTABLE
RAIL JOURNEYS

'Unforgettable' is a funny word. Thanks to countless travel brochures struggling for new superlatives it's taken on a purely positive inference, particularly with rail travel.

The masses are lured onto trains like the Orient Express with promises of 'ten unforgettable nights of romance' and end up disillusioned and out-of-pocket. The truth is, an unforgettable rail journey is one you can never forget, even if you want to. It may be because of the spectacular scenery or because the dining car runs out of coffee. Equally, it may be because of the bore who sits next to you or because of the bizarre reasons in the 10 following examples.

1. Budapest, Hungary to Zagreb, Croatia

It wasn't the scenery that made this a journey I'll never forget. It was the perverted American I met as the Croatian officials interrogated me at the border.

His name was Brad, and as the grim-faced guards flicked through my passport, looking up occasionally to check if I still looked like the photo, Brad detailed his plans to become an international arms dealer. As they searched through my backpack, he confessed to sharing an ancient prostitute in Macedonia with a fellow hosteller. Then, as they returned my backpack, he denied rubbing the breasts of a sixteen-year-old in Prague as the Czech authorities had insisted.

Finally, when the guards were finished with me, Brad tortured me with the details of a decision he had to make—between the pure innocent beauty of 17-year-old Svetlana from Romania or the adulterous charms of 37-year-old Olga from Bratislava.

It's not a long trip from the Hungarian border to Zagreb—but it sure felt like one.

123

2. Tōzai Line, Tokyo Subway

No doubt you've seen the footage of Tokyo's overcrowded subways—with the little guys wearing white gloves scurrying up and down the platform, politely shoving early morning commuters into carriages too full to accept them. But have you noticed how they never show you any footage *inside* the train? That's because, if they did, the Tokyo Subway Authority would be up before the UN Human Rights Commission before you could say 'Aum Doomsday Cult'.

As someone who commuted for close to nine months in Tokyo on the heavily populated Tōzai Line, let me tell you—I'm ready to be the star witness.

3. Kigoma to Dar es Salaam, Tanzania

According to the timetable, the journey from Kigoma, a lakeside town on the far-flung western boundary of Tanzania, to Dar es Salaam on the east coast, takes 36 hours. Unfortunately, African timetables are works of fiction, mythologised accounts of how things may once have been. The duration of a particular journey is a gamble, although two to three times longer than the station master tells you is usually a good bet.

124

Getting a seat beyond Tabora, where the train meets with the train coming south from Mwanza, is also a bit of a lottery. The trick is to track down the station master as soon as the train arrives in Tabora. In keeping with the spirit of things, the station master hides, rewarding those with the cunning and initiative to find him with the best tickets.

I spent a couple of hours dodging shunting trains in the pre-dawn darkness before I eventually found him sitting in an abandoned carriage, doling out the sought-after seat allocations by candlelight.

4. Quetta to Rawalpindi, Pakistan

This train travels through the dry heart of Pakistan, wheezing through areas where even in winter the mercury pushes 30°C. I made the mistake of catching it during one of the country's worst heatwaves.

Thankfully, I managed to secure a hard sleeper for the journey and spent the time lying about half a metre from the roof. Sure, the roof was hot to the touch and the nearest fan was clogged with grime and hadn't worked since the days of Rudyard Kipling but at least I could toss deliriously from side to side and wallow in a pool of my own sweat, rather than the collective pool of the whole carriage.

The only drawback was the guy on the bunk opposite who kept proudly proclaiming in that particularly subcontinental sing-song tone that this was the hottest place in the whole world. I didn't need him to tell me that and promptly silenced him with a quick blow to the head.

125

5. Chihuahua to Los Mochis, Mexico

The Copper Canyon is quite rightly regarded as one of the most spectacular rail journeys in the world. But it wasn't the scenery that made this journey stick in my mind. It was the retired United States admiral who took offence at my bargaining skills in Divisadero, the siding where the train stops for passengers to take a geek at the spectacular canyon and buy a piece of tacky Mexican memorabilia.

He seemed to get particularly bothered when I attempted to lower the stratospheric asking price for a fetching wooden figurine by assuring the stall owner I was not an American—not unreasonable considering the train was 90 per cent full of retired Americans with pension cheques to burn. This admiral spent the rest of the journey demanding to know from which insolent country I came. I refused to say, preferring to hint that I was from a small country of absolutely no significance. 'Oh, so you're a New Zealander', he said, and stormed off, doubtlessly to deploy the USS *Nimitz* just off Auckland.

I would normally defend the honour of my accent in such situations but, hey, my bargaining ploy had worked. The woman gave me the figurine for one-tenth of what she first asked.

6. Banyuwangi to Solo, Indonesia

This was my first trip on a Third World train. As any traveller will tell you, it's one of life's defining moments. I spent the whole day gawping at the scene played out before me, buying whatever trackside hawkers shoved in my face, sharing meals of dubious heritage with friendly passengers, and choking on the stench of a thousand Kretek cigarettes. It took three times longer than the bus, but I wouldn't have missed it for the world.

7. Golmud to Lanzhou, China

This journey through the backwaters of China was my introduction to the oriental habit of having a good old golly.
The train had barely pulled out of Golmud when the
carriage erupted into a cacophony of coughing,
sniffing and sprogging. Within minutes the floor
was awash with the gooey, green spittle of the
travelling classes of Red China. The outside of
the train, just to the back of the open windows
was similarly coated.

What surprised me the most was the extraordinary
depths to which the Chinese go within their bodies to
bring up the last bit of phlegm. I was most surprised that
the mandatory chest infection I came down with wasn't tuberculosis.

8. The Budapest Metro, Hungary

Designed and built by the USSR in the sixties, the
Budapest Metro is a unique blend of Soviet
practicality and Russian extravagance. It was
this spirit that imbued the following incident
with a Cold War resonance.

I was sitting in a carriage minding my own
business at Népstadion, heading back into
the centre of Budapest. The train was
empty except for three men scattered further down the carriage nonchalantly reading
newspapers.

126

The instant the doors slid shut, however, the three
men jumped up and surrounded me, pulling up their jacket sleeves to
reveal the dreaded red armband of the plain-clothes ticket inspector. It had
been such an elaborate and precise sting that I was genuinely sorry that I
had a valid three-day pass in my pocket. The inspectors were pretty disappointed too. They slunk off to another carriage, their spirits broken.

9. Rangoon to Mandalay, Burma

Back in 1986, when the Burmese would only let you into their country for
seven days, missing the train was tantamount to missing the country. So
when the lovely lass at Tourist Burma said that the only way I could get
on the overnight train to Mandalay was to sleep on the floor, I took her
up on the offer.

Being the shy, retiring type I let everyone else settle in before I picked my spot. Not surprisingly, the only spot left was in front of the toilet. I spent the night being stepped on by everyone going into the loo and having the door jammed into my ribs by everyone coming out. Sometime during the night the toilet overflowed and I awoke smelling like a public urinal. I had a lot of space then.

10. Istanbul to Erzurum, Turkey

OK, I admit it. I'm the kind of guy who won't travel first class unless someone else is paying. But when I turned up at Istanbul's Haydarpaşa train station and noticed that I could travel across inflation-racked Turkey for less than A$10, I weakened.

I'm glad I did. I had my own compartment with a bed, crisp clean sheets, a real pillow and a little basin that folded down from the wall with taps that actually worked. And on each of the two mornings I spent aboard, a little man in a neatly pressed uniform brought me a delicious breakfast. Oh, and the scenery was pretty spectacular too.

127

● ●
Honourable mention: Khartoum to Wadi Halfa, Sudan
You know that feeling you get when you think you're going to drown? Well, I had that feeling for close to 50 hours on this train. Except it wasn't water that was stopping me getting my breath, it was dust. When I woke up on the first night unable to breathe, it was the closest I've ever come to jumping out of a moving train. Considering we were in the middle of a desert and it was a once-a-week train, it was probably a good thing that I didn't.
● ●

Chapter 14

BUS ES

Back in the seventies a hippy guru called Ed Buryn described bus travel as being 'funky and outrageous'. Back then, travelling by bus was an experience that overwhelmed your senses and changed your life. It still can be, especially in the backblocks of Asia, the Middle East and South America. In those places buses are 'funky' in the true sense of the word— they inspire fear, panic and cowardice. They're 'outrageous' in that they defy all laws of physics, cramming more humanity into a tin can on wheels than is scientifically possible.

129

In many ways, they're the best thing about travelling.

Why travel by bus?

Next to hitching or walking, buses are the cheapest way of getting from Point A to Point B. What's more, they'll service all the parts in between that trains will not, or cannot, go.

There are drawbacks, however. Most bus companies are private enterprises motivated by only one thing—money. They are hell-bent on getting the most money out of people while spending the least amount possible. As a consequence, buses are unreliable, uncomfortable and overcrowded.

In short, just what every backpacker worth their salt hankers for.

You know you are travelling by bus when ...

Buses are usually big, styleless and have lots of seats. If you're still unsure, check for these telltale signs.

o   The music played loudly over tinny speakers is either heavy metal or easy listening.

o   The vehicle breaks down nine times—before it even gets out of the terminal.

o   The driver goes to change the tyre and remembers that he hasn't fixed the spare since it got buggered on the last trip— or that he hasn't got one.

o   The said vehicle leaves a couple of hours late—or on time, if you're late.

o   After leaving late, the vehicle goes 500 metres before stopping to fill up with petrol.

o   500 metres before you get to your final destination, it will stop for petrol again.

o   The driver looks permanently startled and sniffs a lot.

o   Your pack was last to get put on and the last to come off.

o   If it rains, your pack will be the only thing to get wet. If a rope breaks, your pack will be the only thing to fall off.

o   You wake up halfway through the trip convinced an entire village and their livestock have encamped on your forehead.

o   You discover that they have.

o   You arrive at your destination an hour or so before dawn or just after midnight.

o   The nearest hotel is a $20 taxi ride away.

Why are buses so brightly coloured?

130

Travel anywhere in the Third World and you will be dazzled by the intricate colours and designs that even the most modest of buses are festooned with. You might be tempted into thinking that it is just another manifestation of the pride the owners feel towards their major investment, not unlike regular maintenance and careful scrutiny of prospective bus drivers. Don't.

A closer inspection will reveal that each colour is in fact the result of a different accident. Unable to get the exact colour to match the original duco in these remote areas, the owners use whatever they can get their hands on.

Are all bus drivers mad?

Travel on a bus anywhere in the world, particularly areas with perilously treacherous mountain roads, and you'll be convinced that your driver has either just got out of an asylum or is a bitter individual, hell-bent on destruction and determined to take you down with them.

He has. And he is.

Bus terminals: Which is the right one for me?

In many large cities, particularly in developing countries, you will find that there is often more than one bus terminal. They usually have imaginative names like Bus Terminal East, Bus Terminal West and so on.

Many people fall into the trap of thinking that buses heading east will go from Bus Terminal East and that those heading north will go from Bus Terminal North. While this is sometimes the case, it is not a rule set in concrete.

Rather, think of it this way. It is an unalterable law of nature that the bus terminal you need to go to will be on the opposite side of town to where your hotel or hostel is. It is also inevitable that when you finally get there it will have closed or moved.

How do I get to a bus terminal?

You've paid your bills, you've put your pack on your back and you're off to catch the bus out of there. Logic would dictate that the best way to get to the bus terminal would be by bus.

Not so. These places hate buses. They are designed for inter and intra national bus travel. The last thing they want is some clapped-out municipal bus clogging up the terminal. Besides, they get a better commission from taxi drivers.

131

That is, unless you're somewhere like Istanbul. They have a cheap, regular tram service that runs right by the terminal. But convenience like that doesn't last. The city fathers probably have plans to move the terminal further out and redevelop the old terminal into a housing estate for 230,000 people.

How do I survive a bus terminal?

Barely. Keep your eyes on the ground and do not respond to any of the touts yelling at you, even if their prices seem rather attractive or they claim that the last bus for the week is about to leave. Go instead to the ticket offices and play each of the clerks against each other.

And whatever you do, don't eat anything.

Where is the best place to sit? The front seat?

On any bus the seat that inspires envy amongst other passengers is right up the front on the side opposite the driver. Here, after everyone has boarded, you can lazily dangle your feet into the step well, luxuriating in space denied every other passenger on the bus.

There is also the added bonus of being able to disembark first. At those midnight courtesy stops, you'll be the first one into the toilet. At the meal breaks, you'll be the first to the table to eat. However, considering the state of most bus stop toilets, and the state of most bus stop meals, it is a rather dubious honour.

Of course, there is a downside to all these positives. Being right up front you have nothing ahead of you except for the windscreen—not a good thing during the inevitable head-on collision. Secondly, before that head-on collision, you get to see the near misses that the other passengers staring into the head of the person in front of them fail to see. And finally, when you collapse into a fit of exhausted sleep, you'll be constantly awakened by the glare of oncoming headlights.

Should women refuse the front seat?

If you're a woman and you're offered the seat next to the driver, you should be aware that it is also a trophy chair. When other buses pass it will be naturally assumed that you are the driver's woman—or at least someone he fancies his chances with. While you may not have a problem with this—after all, you know that it's not true—it could impact on you in more direct ways. For example, at every meal stop the driver will come and sit with you.

But that's not the worst of it. On some buses in Indonesia there is a very attractive bench seat, right up front adjacent to the driver. It is not unknown for drivers to surreptitiously grope the girl sitting on the seat every time they change gears.

What about the back seat?

It might have been cool on the bus to school, but it ain't when you're travelling.

A law of physics—I'm not sure which one—states that by the time the effect of a bus hitting a bump, pothole or small animal reaches the back of that said bus it has been magnified to a velocity not dissimilar to that needed to launch the space shuttle—not a good thing when you consider the state of most roads throughout the backpacker's world.

I travelled from Kathmandu to the Indian border on the back seat of a particularly decrepit bus once and such was the state of the road that I was tossed into the roof several times. Only a long conversation with the Canadian girl next to me about the relative merits of Canada's biggest musical exports at that time, Men Without Hats and Martha and the Muffins, saved me from long-term psychological damage.

Don't expect it to be any better if the back seat is packed solid. It just means that the entire row will go up as one demented Mexican wave and land like a madwoman's breakfast.

133

Somewhere in the middle, perhaps?

Life is about compromise and so, too, it is with bus seats. A seat somewhere around the middle will shield you from the bumps of the back and the bright lights and sexual harassment that are par for the course up front.

What it won't do is save you from the claustrophobia, heat and body odour that is part and parcel of travelling by bus. It won't stop the local woman from resting her baby on your shoulder as she changes its shitty nappy. But then, neither does sitting somewhere in the middle of the bus going to work back home.

Bus seats: Velour or vinyl?

Whoah! You're asking the big ones aren't you?

Seriously, though, questions such as these are very important, especially if you are travelling for more than a couple of hours.

First, let's look at vinyl. No one is really sure why vinyl was invented in the first place, let alone used to cover bus seats. In the tropics, particularly in direct sunlight, it is scalding to the touch, it causes you to sweat and, as a totally non-porous material, lets you wallow in your own sweat. Sweat or no sweat, it is not a surface to hold you snug and secure on those winding mountain roads. Don't be surprised if you end up in the aisle or on the lap of the person three rows away.

While velour gives you more grip, it also holds onto food scraps and other less savoury deposits with an alarmingly tenacity. And in the tropics, it really isn't any cooler, the only difference between velour and vinyl being that velour soaks up the sweat.

In short, just put up with what you get, 'cos you ain't gonna to get much choice anyway.

Should I eat roadhouse food?

A feature of any long journey on a coach or bus are the regular stops in little roadside diners to eat and relieve oneself. In Islamic countries they often have a small mosque at the side for the faithful to pray. In Australia, they are usually attached to an oversized creature like a prawn or a ram, set in concrete and towering 20 or 30 metres high.

The quality of the food at these establishments varies from country to country. In some places like Turkey, where the cost of the meal is included in the price of your ticket, it is generally exceptional and tasty. In Indonesia—and the rest of Asia for that matter—it is more of a hit-and-miss affair. Sometimes it's good but usually it is bland, over-priced and served up by the bus driver's mate. In Australia, all you seem to get is deep-fried crap where you pay extra for each of the fourteen times it has been re-fried during the day.

Finally, a word of warning. If you ever have to travel by bus in Albania—and here's hoping you never have to—take your own food with you, preferably from a neighbouring country. I tried to eat a bowl of con-gealed fat at a roadside restaurant there nearly two years ago and I'm still undergoing treatment.

Will I find romance on a bus?

Have you ever stopped to wonder why they set *Before Sunrise* with Ethan Hawke and Julie Delpy on a train and not a bus?

Well, for one thing, the likes of Ethan and Julie don't catch buses that are crowded, smelly and prone to breaking down. And for another, it's a little difficult to impress a girl with a treatise on existentialism when Indonesian heavy metal is screeching out of a speak-er centimetres above your head at mind-melting lev-els. I know it shouldn't be but it is.

So I can't get all philosophical on a bus?

Sure you can. It is more than likely you will spend the long hours between dusk and dawn staring into the darkness pondering the meaning of life. And riding on a crowded bus, penned in by a pack of Turkish chain smokers, does require a certain kind of stoicism.

In fact, I once met a guy who was writing his thesis on bus travel as proof of Descartes famous maxim 'I think therefore I am'. He explained the basic tenets of his argument but I'm afraid I couldn't quite under-stand what he was getting at. But then, I couldn't understand why he changed his name to Click East either.

TOP 10 HORRIFIC BUS RIDES

What is it that makes a bad bus trip so much harder to endure than a shocking flight or a tiresome train journey? Is it the fact that, unlike flying, you can spend 24 hours on a bus and still not have put some substantial kilometres behind you? Or perhaps it's because, unlike on a train, a walk down the aisle is likely to see you catapulted through the front windscreen. Maybe it is rather more individual reasons like the ones in the 10 horror stories below.

1.   Denpasar, Bali to Probolinggo, Java

I didn't notice this vehicle at first. I just thought it was a bus waiting to be towed away to the wreckers. It was only when the driver fired it up and everyone clambered on board that I realised it was capable of movement.

After checking and double checking my ticket, I realised with horror that it was the bus that was meant to take me to Probolinggo, more than eight hours away.

As the bus wheezed its way onto the road to a soundtrack of excruciatingly bad Indonesian heavy metal music at mind numbingly loud levels, I sat clutching my ears and wondered if I should give up the idea of travelling and go home right there and then.

When the head gasket blew barely 35 kilometres up the road I knew I should have.

2.   Lago Agrio to Quito, Ecuador

This is a long trip but thankfully it was mostly uneventful—that is, until we cleared the highest road pass in the world and made our descent into Quito.

Quito looked so beautiful—a glittering bowl of fairy lights below—that at first I didn't notice that the bus had emptied of everyone except for me and the bus driver. I was then confused by the fact that the bus hadn't stopped. Just when I had convinced myself that the passengers had all been taken by the Secret Rapture, I saw them grabbing rocks and throwing them under the wheels. Then I noticed the driver, crunching down through the gears and pumping furiously on the brakes.

Thankfully, a few of the more forward-thinking passengers ran ahead and, with the help of a large branch, levered a boulder the size of a small car into the path of the bus. It seemed to do the trick.

3.   Mwanza to Busisi, Tanzania

This journey opened my eyes to just how insatiable some Africans are. I was innocently sitting in my chair (coincidentally held in an upright position by a rope tied to the chair in front) when a rather attractive lass sashayed up to the guy in front, hitched her skirt and promptly mounted him.

I should point out that she wasn't one of these types that lays back and thinks of Tanzania either. The rope was twanging with such a velocity that I thought it was going to snap and have my eye out.

4.   Sydney to Brisbane, Australia

It's funny, but when I travel overseas I seem to be able to cope with sitting on a bus for sixteen hours straight without losing too much of my sanity. But when I have to do it back home—in buses that would be the envy of most other countries and on roads that are reasonably good—I end up having to undergo therapy.

I guess being forced to eat in restaurants attached to the 'Big Prawn' or the 'Big Oyster' doesn't help. And nor does the knowledge that, at the end of it all, there isn't an exotic city laden with the pungent aromas of spices and sewage—just Brisbane.

137

5.   Taftan to Quetta, Pakistan

Ever had that sinking feeling when you buy a bus ticket that when you board the bus you'll find a village of smelly but colourfully dressed gypsies encamped in your seat with all their goods and chattels and steadfastly determined not to move?

I did when I bought my ticket on this ride from the Iranian border to Quetta. And you know what? It turned out to be true.

6. London, England, to Prague, Czech Republic

The driver of this bus had the unfortunate distinction of looking exactly like Eddie Van Halen. And he drove the bus as I imagine Eddie Van Halen would drive a 50-seater coach—right into the back of an Austin Metro on the big roundabout at Elephant and Castle barely five minutes from the Victoria Coach Station.

Thankfully, the driver ran off into the night before the police arrived and was replaced by the conductor. She may have looked like an East German swimmer, but at least she got us to Prague safe and sound.

7. Sintang to Nanga Pinoh, Kalimantan

I would never have believed it possible to take five hours to travel 35 kilometres but that was before I took this bus trip from hell. I never knew the true meaning of agony either until I sat on my seat on the same bus and had my posterior pierced by a particularly poor piece of welding.

8. Tierradentro to Mocoa, Colombia

When I flagged down this bus in the pre-dawn drizzle, little did I know what I was letting myself in for. Squeezed onto a bench, with the canvas windows rolled down and the humidity way up, I quaked with fear along with my fellow passengers as the bus clung precariously to a freshly graded road that clung just as precariously to the side of the Andes.

There was a happy ending though. When I arrived in Mocoa, a rather friendly army patrol escorted me to a hotel and insisted the owner take me in—at a very attractive rate. Due to my catatonic state at the time, I rather rudely forgot to thank them.

9.   Dali to Kunming, China

In China they have this rather nifty notion with buses. Take out all the seats, cram it with bunk beds, and call it a 'Sleeper Bus'. Before you know it, backpackers are falling over themselves to travel long distances at over-the-odds prices in the mistaken belief they'll get a decent night's sleep.

Not surprisingly, it doesn't work that way. The bunks are Chinese size, meaning that they are a couple of feet shy even for a short person like me. What's more, the roof is so low that those on the top bunk have their noses squashed against the ceiling. I got so claustrophobic that I pushed open the air vent above me, even though it was monsoonal outside, just to get a couple of extra inches for my nose.

10.   Split, Croatia, to Mostar, Bosnia

You know when you do something on the spur of the moment without thinking it through properly and then spend the rest of your life regretting it? Well, this bus trip was a bit like that. I saw a bus heading to Mostar in war-torn Bosnia and though it would be a neat idea to catch it.

I spent the next eight hours fingering the bullet holes in the window beside my seat, getting interrogated by both Croatian and Bosnian officials as to what the hell I was doing going to Mostar, and gawking at bombed bridges and devastated apartment blocks.

To top it all off, I arrived in Mostar at dusk only to be told that the only hotel in town was a mortar-punctured shell and that the next bus back to Split was in three days. Not one of my best decisions, that's for sure.

139

140

Nothing quite captures the sense of adventure or the allure of the unknown like a boat. Fragile yet fearless, boats have taken mankind beyond the edge of the world to new lands and new lives.

As a backpacker in far-flung lands they will take you to long forgotten corners too. They will take you up rivers and across oceans, up tributaries and around harbours. And if you're really lucky, they'll also take you to within an inch of your life.

141

Why boats?

Well, to be honest, if you find yourself in the position to catch a boat in your travels, it's probably because there's no other way of getting to where you want to go.

But that's not such a bad thing. Boats are probably the most leisurely and relaxing way of getting from A to B. Should they get stuck on a sand bank or get blown off course by a storm, they'll be even more so.

Travelling by boat in the Third World: Some inevitabilities

Although no two boat rides are ever the same, each being a unique little adventure of its own, there are some things about hitting the high seas in the Third World that never change. For example:

o There will be more passengers than life jackets.

o Any life jacket on the boat will be snapped up immediately to be used as a pillow or an item of high fashion.

o The lowering mechanism on the lifeboat has seized up. Worse still, it has long ago become home to an extended family of sea terns or Russian stowaways.

- You finally find your reserved bunk on a Pelni passenger ship in Indonesia only to discover that an entire Indonesian family have set up the charcoal cooker and claimed it as their spiritual home.
- The kitchen will run out of food just as you arrive at the window with your tray. On seeing what everyone else was doled up, you will be eternally grateful.
- You will be overwhelmed by the smell of diesel fumes—even if it is a sail boat.
- Your captain will consider the Plimsoll line as being purely decorative.

How can I avoid seasickness?

I'm really the wrong person to be asking about this. Anything rougher than a bathtub and I'm doubled over the rails making burley. Which is a shame really because as a Cancerian I have this fatal attraction to the sea that makes me forget all this and go by boat whenever I can—with dire consequences.

What I have discovered, though, is the importance of air circulation. If it's hot and stuffy, I'm really struggling. Throw in a whiff of diesel and I'm a goner. But if I get a bit of a breeze on my sweaty brow I can usually keep the diced carrot at bay for a couple of hours at least.

142

When is it most dangerous on a boat?

That moment on a chosen mode of transport when you have really put your life at risk comes early with boats. Whereas with airplanes it's when you're taking off and landing and with buses it's the moment the terrorist bomb goes off, with boats it's the moment you try to get on board.

How can I board a boat with dignity?

You can't. From the most modest of dugout canoes to the grandest of liners, that moment of embarkation is designed specifically to provide the maximum entertainment value for the crew and the onlookers onshore.

Take a dugout canoe for instance. I defy any backpacker to get on board without tipping the bloody thing over and ending up in the drink. Similarly, if they are burdened with a pack laden with Spam and souvenirs, I'd pay good money to see them extricate themselves from the muddy bottom.

It's the same with bigger boats and ships too. On the huge Pelni passenger liners that ply between the innumerable islands of Indonesia it is impossible to survive the God-almighty crush to board with all your limbs—let alone any self-respect.

Where is the best place to spend a boat trip?

It really depends on the boat. If it's small enough, nothing beats sitting up front and dangling your feet overboard. If it's bigger, try somewhere on deck where you can keep out of the sun and get a bit of a breeze to ward off the evils of seasickness.

143

If you're travelling in Indonesia, don't follow the lead of the locals. They inevitably make for the most cramped, airless corner of the boat and then spend the rest of the journey throwing up.

Of course, you could follow the example set by a couple of English girls I met in Asia. They'd search out the captain, flirt with him a little and spend the whole trip on the bridge being brought tea and biscuits and the occasional three-course meal.

Should I eat boat food?

Not unless you have some kind of death wish. From the ferries that ply the English Channel to the boats popping between the islands of Indonesia, it is universally bad. On the channel ferries it is bland and expensive. In Indonesia, you'll be struggling to identify it and if you do, you'll rather wish you hadn't. I dug around a seemingly innocuous bowl of rice once and discovered a fish head. Alarmingly, it was missing its eyeballs.

Is all boat food that bad?

You're right. I am being a little unfair. While some of the
worst meals I have ever had have been on boats, so
have some of the best meals I've ever had travelling.
On a boat taking cars down the Mekong River to
Vientiane in Laos I shared a delicious meal with the
captain's family. Though I'm still not 100 per cent
sure what it was that I was eating, it was delicious
and matched the mood of the Mekong rather nicely.

144

Should I take food with me then?

Yes. And always take more than you think you'll need. Boats have an
unnerving ability of taking much longer than you think and, unlike trains,
there aren't any platforms in the middle of the ocean populated by wal-
lahs with nothing better to do than sell you drinks and snacks at ridiculously low prices.

I got caught out rather badly when I caught a barge down the Zaire River
from Kisangani to Kinshasa. I rather foolishly believed the captain when
he told me the trip would only take six days, and only bought enough rotten avocados and bread to cover a couple of days. It ended up taking six
weeks and only the kindness of the captain's wife saved me from starv-
ing to death. I don't know what I would have done without the dregs of
her husband's fish stew. I might have had to eat the char-grilled monkey
offered by passing locals in canoes.

Tell me about the 'romance of the sea'

You mean all that 'cry of the gull and
tang of sea spray' stuff? It sounds
like you've been reading too many
Joseph Conrad novels. Either that
or you have some repressed fixa-
tions with Old Spice advertise-
ments.

Believe me, there's nothing romantic
about cowering in a corner with a couple of thousand other hapless souls during
a force 10 hurricane or trying to sleep in a
cabin awash with vomit and food scraps.

There are magic moments though, aren't there?

Don't get me wrong. Travelling by boat is probably the most rewarding of journeys a backpacker can undertake. Each journey, no matter how frightening or dangerous, will be filled with moments that you will remember for the rest of your life.

Like that bewitching hour just before dawn when the sky is pink and flying fish are skipping across the sheen of a platinum sea. Or lying on the roof of a boat wending its way up an untamed river late at night basking in the glow of a billion stars that look close enough to touch. Or that most magical of moments—when land finally comes into view after a long treacherous journey.

What about dolphins? Will I see dolphins?

Of course you will. There is an international convention insisting that dolphins gambol with any boat that comes within a kilometre of them. In fact, the only thing coming between you and the absolute certainty of seeing a dolphin is the odd Japanese driftnet fisherman.

Organised boat trips: Are they worth the money?

Anywhere there is water, you'll find a crusty old seafarer offering to take you to a hidden cove or a little-visited island for the cost of a small family sedan. Before you take up his generous offer you should realise that the only thing hidden about the cove is its charms and the reason that locals stopped visiting the island is because it's overrun with tourists.

That's not to say there's not the odd organised boat trip that represents reasonable value for money. Some of the tours out of Kaş on Turkey's Mediterranean coast throw in quite a tasty seafood barbecue. On the boat trips out of Nha Trang in Vietnam, the

145

visit to a decrepit fish farm—where fish are left flapping on the shore when the tide goes out and a pair of schizophrenic turtles pass the time of day frantically chasing each other—is worth the price of the trip alone.

What about crewing?

It sounds like a great idea, doesn't it. Hook up with a yacht sailing around the Mediterranean, through Asia or around the islands of the South Pacific, offer your services as a crew member and get to see the world for nothing—or perhaps even get paid for it.

How sad, then, that it hardly ever works out that way. The decent captains with decent boats have long ago figured out that there are people silly enough to pay for the privilege of hoisting sails and scrubbing decks. And the ones who haven't are individuals who have been on the high seas just a little too long. Worse still, so have all their psychoses.

146

TOP 10 BUMMER BOAT TRIPS

When I sat down to write this top 10, a particularly profound thought struck me: boats are the only mode of transport with safety equipment that might actually do you some good!

You think about it. An oxygen mask isn't going to help when your jet drops from the sky and crashes into an apartment block. And a seat belt is pretty useless if your bus plummets down a ravine and bursts into flames. Yet a life raft—or even a life jacket—would come in mighty handy if and when your boat sinks.

Why is it then that most boats don't have them? Or if they do, why are they either few in number or defective? I just thought I'd share that thought with you before telling you about the 10 most death-defying boat trips I've ever survived.

1.   Libreville, Gabon to São Tomé, São Tomé

Already overcrowded to start with, this boat became terminally so when six stowaways emerged from the depths of the engine room covered in grime and sweat barely fifteen minutes out of Libreville.

Thankfully the guys were insurgents and after half an hour of trying to wriggle between families and squat on small children, they decided to go and play with the cache of Chinese 'Flying Goose' rifles they had smuggled aboard with them. They spent the rest of the trip with their legs dangling over the bow taking pot shots at the dolphins that had made the mistake of choosing our boat to gambol with.

147

2. Fuamulaku to Male, the Maldives

Fuamulaku is one of the largest islands in the Maldives and the one closest to the equator. Unfortunately, it is also one of the few islands in the archipelago without a port or pier. The fortnightly boat to Male just anchors offshore and a flotilla of rowboats ferries the passengers and goods.

The day I left Fuamulaku there was quite a carnival atmosphere. The locals were taunting the island's mad girl who was bound and gagged on the beach, and she obliged by kicking sand at them. I was so engrossed that I told my friend Sean to get the first rowboat out with all our gear and that I'd join him later.

Later almost never came. That first boat out failed to get past the initial wave and sank. The mad girl sat on the beach rocking backwards and forwards cackling through her gag as the rest of Fuamulaku rushed into the water to save the passengers and their belongings.

In case you're wondering, Sean survived. But his glasses didn't. After a fruitless search with a mask and snorkel, one of the locals assured Sean that 'the fish are wearing them now'.

3. Dabo to Jambi, Indonesia

With over 13,677 different land masses in their archipelago, you'd think that the Indonesians would have this island-hopping business down to a fine art. If this boat trip was anything to go by, however, they still have a lot to learn.

The first thing they've got to learn is to not go for the first cramped, airless bunk they happen upon. Secondly, when the rough seas and diesel fumes inevitably take their toll, they've got to learn to never, ever throw up all over my pack!

4. Boracay to Manila, the Philippines

You know those really windy days when seagulls are picked up and thrown against plate glass windows whenever they try to fly? Well, this boat trip was a bit like that. Except it wasn't seagulls that were being tossed about, it was people—and they weren't even trying to fly. In fact, most were just sitting in their seats. I guess tropical cyclones tend to have that effect.

5. Kisangani to Kinshasa, Zaire

If I had to nominate the worst six weeks of my life, this would have to be it. Sitting on a barge floating down the Zaire River for 42 days with no food, no drink and no batteries for my Walkman. I have never felt more pathetic, more trapped or more bored in my life. Not even the thrilling prospect of eating my first char-grilled monkey helped.

149

6. Around Halong Bay, Vietnam

Halong Bay in northern Vietnam is rightly regarded as one of the country's foremost natural wonders—a crystal clear bay with over 3000 limestone islands rising majestically towards the sky. Such is the scope of this natural wonder that most tour boats take a couple of days to do the rounds, calling into secluded coves and caves. Ours did it in a couple of hours. That's because we were on the wrong boat with the wrong captain looking for the right boat with the right captain. Then when we found him, rain set in for the remainder of our trip.

Only a spectacular storm—with thunder echoing around the bay as the lightning lit up each pinnacle— saved it from being a total disaster. Well, that and the stash of ridiculously cheap Vietnamese vodka we'd smuggled on board.

7. Padang to Siberut, Indonesia

I don't know what it is about Indonesians, but they seem to have a penchant for using the least suitable boat for any given journey. This boat was a tall one, over three storeys high, and extremely narrow—a design more suitable for cruising along a deep calm river than ploughing through the notoriously rough passage between Padang and Siberut.

About an hour out of Padang the boat began listing as treacherously as I had suspected it might. First it dipped its entire port side into the boiling sea—cleansing the lower deck of vomit and food scraps and the occasional passenger—and then it dipped its starboard side and finished off those passengers silly enough to think they could avoid being drenched by rushing to the other side. For a few minutes the boat righted itself, lulling those who had survived into a false sense of security before starting the whole process all over again. Who says Mother Nature doesn't have a sense of humour?

8. Belém to Manaus, Brazil

The boats that ply the Amazon don't have cabins, nor do they have bunks. They just have huge bare decks with hooks to hang your hammock on.

Now at first this sounds wonderful and romantic—kicking back and rocking as the most famous river in the world passes you by. But with the amount of hammocks they pack in, it ended up like one of those desktop toys so popular in the seventies—the ones with suspended balls that clacked against each other. Instead of a ball setting off a chain reaction, however, it was the antics of the boat's resident hooker down one end that caused an equal, opposite and surprisingly violent reaction down the other.

9. Aore to Malekula, Vanuatu

Tackled late at night in a boat that would fit in most bathtubs—and with only a torch and a compass to guide us—this was perhaps the most foolhardy journey I've ever made. By rights, my life should have ended that dark and stormy night. And, by rights, it should have scared the travel bug right out of me. Thankfully, it only made it worse.

10. Mandalay to Pagan, Burma

Like the Indonesians, the Burmese still have a lot to learn about boat design in its applied form. This deep-bowed boat was an ocean-goer from way back and was not at all suited for the notoriously shallow Irrawaddy River. Almost as if to prove this point, it spent the entire journey lurching from one sand bar to another.

150

Which was fine for a day and a half. My fellow passengers were friendly and generous, and the view from a particularly sticky sandbar just out of Pagan was not unpalatable. But when the beer ran out, so did I—on one of the passing long boats eminently more suited for the journey.

Chapter 16

OTHER MODES OF TRANSPORT

One of the most wonderful things about travelling in some of the more underdeveloped regions of the world is the opportunity you'll get to ride on things you wouldn't even dream of mounting back home. Whether it's a llama or a belching tuk-tuk, one thing is for certain—you'll never be left stranded. If it moves—and you offer its owner enough money—you'll be taken wherever you want to go.

What *is* the most common form of transport?

It's a no-contest really. From the humid hills of Rwanda to the dry, dusty deserts of Afghanistan, one mode of transport is more prevalent than all others—the ubiquitous Japanese mini-van. In Indonesia they're called 'bemos'. In Africa they're called 'matatus'. And in all countries they have the same magical quality of being able to squeeze more people in than is humanly possible.

Well known, but little-studied, mini-van phenomena

On first glance, the Japanese mini-vans found in the less developed regions of the world look the same as any others—a little more battered and rust-riddled to be sure, but not unlike the kind favoured by electricians and plumbers back home. Put them in an exotic locale, however, where the roads are bad and the air heavy with humidity, and they develop characteristics that I'm sure their manufacturers never intended. For example:

o Although designed to service routes without enough passengers to justify using larger buses, a mini-van is unable to leave before it is carrying the equivalent of two busloads of passengers.

151

- Mini-vans have two departure times: minutes *before* you arrive and a couple of hours after.

- No matter how full a mini-van appears, it will wait at least an hour in the tropical sun before leaving. If you leave the van to sit in some shade or get a cold drink, its driver will demand that you get back into the van, insisting that it is about to leave. Needless to say, it doesn't.

- The driver will spend a good part of that hour trying to convince you to 'charter' the entire mini-bus. If you agree, he will spend the next hour circling the town looking for more passengers, who he will insist are his family or friends.

- As with its larger cousin, the bus, within the first kilometre of the journey the mini van will instinctively pull into a service station for petrol.

- Like buses, each mini-van comes with an incredibly loud, but extremely poor quality sound system as a standard feature.

- Mini-van drivers have worse taste in music than bus drivers.

- Moments into any journey, the mini-van will get a flat tyre. Rather than pay for it to be repaired by the mechanic only metres away, the driver will spend the rest of the day waving down other mini-vans for a spare.

- The person in the most awkward position in the mini-van—invariably just under your right buttock—decides to get out and causes a major disturbance in order to do so. One hundred metres down the road, the guy sitting next to him will decide to do the same.

- The guy collecting the money hasn't got the correct change and indicates that he will give it to you after everyone else has paid. When you remind him at the end of the journey he rather convincingly pretends that he doesn't understand what you are saying.

- The contortions needed to squeeze into the already overcrowded vehicle will convince you that you are trialling a new form of torture or at the very least a new game, Travel Twister.

Taxis: The world's second most common form of transport

Arrive at an airport or a train station in any foreign country and you might be tempted into thinking that it is taxis rather than Japanese mini-vans that are the most ubiquitous form of transport in the world of travel. With the inevitable long line of taxis snaking off towards the horizon, it would be a tough case for any jury.

However, this silly idea will be knocked out of your head late on the first night of your trip when you're drunk, the last train for the night has gone and your hostel on the other side of town is about to be locked up for the evening.

153

How can I ensure that a taxi driver isn't ripping me off?

You can't. Providing that you can *find* a taxi when you want to use one, you'll just have to accept it as one of those unpleasant facts of life, like bank fees and senile dementia. Taxi drivers the world over have been specially trained to extract the maximum fare from any person over any given distance.

Isn't there *anything* I can do?

You could try insisting that the taxi driver use the meter on his dash-board. Most will argue that it is broken or it is there simply for decorative purposes, but if you harangue them long enough, they'll put it on. However, experience has taught me that it doesn't make a difference. In fact, it can make matters worse.

On my first trip to Istanbul I arrived well after midnight and was forced to catch a taxi into town. The taxi driver wanted the equivalent of A$15, I offered $5 like my guidebook suggested, and we reached a bit of an impasse. Finally, as a compromise, I got him to put the meter on. Just to spite me, the driver took me on a rather circuitous route to the centre of Istanbul, past the city walls, over the Galata Bridge around the Galata Tower and back again. When he finally dumped me in Sultanahmet the fare came to exactly $15. Only his cheery commentary on all the sights we had passed stopped me from hitting him.

What about the set fare taxis that are available from some airports now?

In theory, a great idea. Instead of haggling with a gaggle of taxi drivers in the humid, fetid carpark you take the rather more civilised approach of buying a pre-paid coupon to your destination from a counter within the air-conditioned confines of the airport.

Sadly, the reality is that it doesn't make that much difference. The rip-off prices have just been institutionalised. In fact, in countries like Bangladesh you end up paying more. Rather than just a greedy driver, you have a greedy middle man to deal with as well.

154   What are tuk-tuks?

Tuk-tuks are three-wheeled, bug-shaped conveyances driven by possessed demons intent on ending their own life and taking you, and the whole planet, with them. They should be avoided at all costs.

The name 'tuk-tuk' supposedly comes from the noise that emanates from these little two-stroke monsters. It makes them sound cute and cuddly and infers that riding in them is a soothing experience akin to an hour or so in a flotation tank. Nothing could be further from the truth. It's just that the Thai people had a hard time coming up with a name that encapsulated the tuk-tuk experience—although 'those ugly, unroadworthy, fume-belching, life-threatening, limb-crunching, overpriced things with three wheels that sound like a jackhammer on speed' goes pretty close.

If you ever do have to use one, I hope for your sake that it doesn't crash. I once saw one roll in Thailand and it put me off them for life. As it sat spinning on its roof on one of Bangkok's busiest thoroughfares it reminded me of a turtle turned on its back. But then that could have just been the effect of the limbs of the driver and his passengers thrashing about wildly as they tried to get out of the wreckage.

And rickshaws?

Rickshaws are bicycles with a bench seat, modified especially to allow certain crazy individuals to eke out a rather pathetic existence cycling people short distances around a town.

Even when a rickshaw wallah is ripping you off blind, rickshaws are an obscenely cheap way of getting around. Understandably, many of the more politically enlightened travellers have a problem with a fellow human being pedalling them around. Just remember that many successful tuk-tuk drivers and mini-van owners started their careers as a rickshaw wallah. What's more, rickshaws are much friendlier on the environment than your average tuk-tuk or mini-van.

Me and my backpack weigh a tonne. Won't I kill the rickshaw wallah?

The first thing you have to do is get over this feeling of guilt. So what if you're seven or eight times the weight of his usual passengers? Your rickshaw wallah has already factored this into his calculations by charging you seven or eight times the price he charges everyone else. So sure, he might knock himself out pedalling you up to that hillside pagoda, but with the amount he'll earn he'll be able to take the rest of the week off to recover.

Having said that, if you plan to travel more than a couple of kilometres, consider a tuk-tuk. For everyone's sake.

Do they still use animals for transport in some countries?

In some of the poorer countries, including northern England, commuters are still forced to use animals to get them down to the shops or to and from work. As a rule they are cheaper to buy and maintain than a Japanese mini-van, and when they're past their use-by date, their owners can eat them.

When should *I* use an animal as transport?

Who amongst us hasn't dreamed of crossing the Andes by llama or traipsing across some hostile desert on the back of a camel? Unfortunately, after a couple of minutes on either of these animals you will understand why they invented bucket seats with velour trim.

That's why it's best to use animals for short journeys or colourful photo opportunities. That way you get to satiate your wild adventurer fantasies and the folks back home get to have a good laugh.

155

A word of warning: Try to keep your cowboy instincts under control when sitting on an animal. A misplaced 'Ye-hah!' is often all it takes to get the camel you're sitting on galloping off into the desert—with you on the back—never to be seen again.

Should I consider catching a truck?

In many of the more remote corners of the globe, the only ways to get between Point A and Woop Woop is to walk or catch a truck. Now, at first this may seem an eminently sensible idea but there are problems.

Firstly, trucks are not designed to carry people. They are designed to carry inanimate objects that don't mind being roughly thrown about. After a couple of weeks travelling in bemos and the like, you may well be tempted to think that sounds rather like you. Don't. Truck travel, combined with unbelievably bad roads, is designed to make you remember you're alive, if only to have you wishing you had never been born.

I remember one particular journey in Kalimantan, where the driver had thoughtfully placed two planks of wood across a row of forty-four gallon drums for passengers to sit on. Rather than making the trip more comfortable, his 'thoughtfulness' made the journey worse. The elevated position meant that I spent a lot of the time swatting off low-lying branches. And the bumping road meant that I spent the rest of the time screaming in pain as various parts of my anatomy got squished between the planks and the drums when they came back down to rest.

What about riding in the cabin?

Even if you're lucky enough to secure a seat in the cabin, you'll come across the other major problem with trucks—truck drivers. They tend to be rather coarse individuals who will spend

156

the entire journey spaced out or drunk or trying to grope you. They also have a habit of choosing places to stay on the basis of whether there is a brothel attached. In Africa they also have the disconcerting habit of valuing a ride in the cabin well beyond its real worth. Once I scored a lift with a particularly disreputable fellow across the north of Zaire who tried to hit me for US$40, roughly the same as an airfare for the same journey would have cost. I jumped in the back with the locals and only had to shell out $10.

What about walking?

While hiking and trekking can be extremely enjoyable experiences, walking as a means of getting from A to B is not. That's because it's not something you choose to do. Rather it's something that is forced upon you when there are no buses or trains and when none of the bastards driving past in their cars are willing to stop. Inevitably, it will turn out a longer traipse than you imagined and the weather will turn foul on you.

The only two occasions I have been forced to walk have been disastrous. On the Isle of Arran in Scotland I got caught in a thunderstorm and spent the afternoon huddling under a ledge with smelly sheep. The other time, I discovered that the longest known measurement in the universe is the distance from the last town in Serbia to the first town in Bulgaria.

157

Hitching?

To be honest, I haven't had much experience with hitching, mainly because I think of what state I'd have to be in to pick up a scruffy backpacker standing beside the road waving his thumb at me, and decide against it.

The few times that I have indulged in hitchhiking have only served to confirm this. On the road to Skopje in Macedonia I was picked up by a family of mad Albanians who promptly started biting and hitting each other. In Kenya I was picked up by a drunk called Elvis who proceeded to tell me his rather pathetic life story as he wove all over the road, eventually knocking a policeman off his bike and into a ditch.

But I have heard stories of travellers who have been picked up by drivers who travel thousands of kilometres out of their way for them, buy them meals and introduce them to their nymphomaniacal offspring. But I have always tended to put these stories in the same category as the stories about free love ashrams in India and cheap airfares in Australia—the category especially created for the mad hallucinations of a traveller who has been too long on the road.

The NSITT guide to *other* other modes of transport

Of course, the modes of transport I have mentioned are but a few of the many transport options you'll be confronted with in your travels. Even a cursory discussion of each would fill an entire book. Rather than leave you ill-prepared for the frightening amount of choices you'll have, here's a quick guide to some of the more common choices that will be available.

Hired driver and car

Pros: You get to sit back and lord it over the locals, waving occasionally in the manner preferred by the pope and the royal family.

Cons: You'll pay dearly for the privilege and you'll see more of the insides of craft shops and crappy roadside restaurants than you will of the sights.

Self-drive (motorcycle or car)

Pros: You won't be forced against your will into craft shops, cafes or poor quality theme parks.

Cons: Local law enforcement officers will feel compelled to fine you or extract large sums of money from you as bribes for real or imaginary traffic violations. There is also a very real possibility of the loss of limbs or at the very least, a layer of skin or two.

158

Horse and cart

Pros: A very picturesque and romantic way to see the sights. Guaranteed to sway even the most reluctant of companions to things amour.

Cons: In the West, even the shortest of rides necessitates a rather substantial loan. In the East, the poor diet of horses means it can be a rather smelly experience.

Bicycles

Pros: A rambling, relaxing way to soak up the sights and sounds of any given destination.

Cons: The quickest way to realise how unfit you are and that you *can* forget how to ride a bike, usually in front of an oncoming bus.

Motorcycle taxis

Pros: Quick, cheap, convenient and you don't have to wait for it to fill up before it goes.

Cons: Lack of regulation in the motorcycle taxi industry means that the average motorcycle taxi driver is just a guy with a bike who needs a couple of extra dollars to take his girlfriend to the movies. His knowledge of where you want to go reflects this.

Bicycle taxis

Pros: None known.

Cons: As with motorcycle taxis, except the owners are younger and probably just after the money for a candy bar.

159

TOP 10
TIRESOME
JOURNEYS

Unusual modes of transport have a particularly strong hold on the imagination of travellers. There's something undeniably romantic about the thought of riding a camel through the deserts of Baluchistan or hitching a ride across the tangled interior of Africa in a truck. But, believe me, in reality the novelty soon wears off. Here's 10 times it wore off rather quickly.

1. The Valley of the Kings by donkey, Luxor, Egypt

The Valley of the Kings is a good nine or ten kilometres across dry, dusty desert and crumbling, barren mountains from Luxor. God only knows why I thought it would be a good idea to hire a donkey to take me there.

My donkey was a particularly little fellow, so small in fact that my feet could easily touch the ground when I sat on his back. I spent a good part of the day just getting to the first tomb, my knees tucked under my chin. On arriving I promptly abandoned the donkey and hired a taxi.

2. Pegu by horse and cart, Burma

Pegu is a charming little town about 80 kilometres from Rangoon. It's renowned for its exquisite pagodas and one of the largest reclining Buddhas in Asia. The town is small enough, and the sights close enough, to get around on foot but I was rather taken by the romantic notion of gadding about by horse and cart. Unfortunately, 10 minutes into my grand tour, the horse pulling my cart collapsed from exhaustion and malnutrition and the owner was too upset to continue.

160

3. Equator monument by motor-cycle taxi, Bontang, Indonesia

Keen to see the world-famous equator monument of Bontang—well, maybe not *that* keen—I secured the services of one of the lads hanging around with their motorcycles at the bus station. Although the guy assured me that he had been to the monument before, he hadn't, and instead showed me more of Bontang while looking for it than anyone wanting to keep their sanity should. After six hours under the fearsome equatorial sun we finally found the monument, a mere 10 minutes out of town. When I was deposited back at the bus station, the guy had the hide to ask for extra money for the 'tour'. I told him to bugger off.

4. Rwandan border by petrol tanker, Tanzania

Riding in a petrol tanker across central Africa, the smell of crude oil and ugali in my nostrils, had never been one of my travelling fantasies. It was just that I had missed the only bus traversing the 150 kilometres from Mwanza in Tanzania to the Rwandan border, and it was the first means of transport to come along. I spent the next five days bouncing along moonscape roads, swatting tsetse flies and helping the drivers repair twisted differentials and cracked heads. They were the longest 150 kilometres of my life.

5. Ute scootin' around Somalia

I spent the good part of a week driving around war-torn Somalia with some guys in a 'requisitioned' international aid ute with a machine gun welded to the roof. It was kind of fun hooning around the scrubby plains of southern Somalia, pointing refugees towards the Kenyan border and just generally having a good old paddock bash. Then the thought crossed my mind that they might actually have to use the machine gun and it suddenly lost all of its appeal.

161

6. Jinja to Lake Victoria by bicycle taxi, Uganda

With bugger all else to do in this forgettable town east of Kampala, the group I was travelling with decided to go down to the Gentleman's Club on the shores of Lake Victoria. There were mini-vans doing the journey, but we thought it would be more fun to go with some of the young lads offering to take us on the back of their bicycles. The fun stopped after the second kilometre and the sore bums began.

7. Oysha to Komanda by ute, Zaire

I made the mistake of hesitating when this ute pulled up in Oysha on its way north to Komanda. Within seconds it was full and I was left with the unenviable position of sitting in the back right-hand corner with a bamboo pole between my legs. At first I amused myself by pretending it was a joystick and I was somehow in control of the car's movements. One rather nasty bump that severely damaged my ability to father children soon put paid to that little game.

8. Amber Fort by elephant, India

There's a long, winding pathway that leads from the roadside entrance of Amber Fort to the magnificent palace at the top. For a small fee you can make the journey on a suitably prissied up elephant. For a considerably larger fee, their enterprising owners will make the elephant kneel down so you can get off.

9. Cayambe to Mount Cayambe by Ford F100, Ecuador

162

The owner of this rather dilapidated Ford pickup truck assured us that his vehicle was more than capable of making the torturous journey through the Andean highlands to the Refugio on the slopes of Mount Cayambe—even with the massive bundles of firewood we had bought for the occasion. What he failed to tell us was that it was also eminently capable of getting bogged a good seven kilometres short, leaving us with 20 kilos of firewood and severely out of breath.

10. Riding on a camel in Giza, Egypt

During my stay in Egypt I became quite adept at riding camels. I even got to the stage of getting them to obey most of my commands. Unfortunately, I was less successful with their owners. They insisted on spoiling my Lawrence of Arabia fantasies by invariably demanding 35 times the price we had agreed on at the beginning of our journey.

Chapter 17

BORDER CROSSINGS

Coming from an island nation, I have always found border crossings strange and fascinating beasts. Where I come from, if you want to go to another country you jump on a plane, not a bus. Perhaps that's why whenever I come across a land border I have this childish desire to put one foot in each country or at the very least go 'Now I'm in Switzerland and now I'm in France, now I'm in Switzerland and now I'm in France'. But I digress. This topic is designed to give you the dirt on crossing from one country to another—with the maximum of fuss and the most hassles possible.

What is a border crossing?

A border is an arbitrary line drawn on a map between two countries. It sometimes marks a quite distinct division in politics, religion and financial well-being, but mostly it is an ill-conceived line that is designed to give two very similar peoples something to fight about for centuries.

A border crossing is a point along that line where people are permitted to cross from one country into the other. What matters most to travellers, however, is that on either side of the said crossing is a border post. These border posts will invariably be manned by ill-tempered, voraciously greedy individuals whose sole purpose is to make the process of crossing from one country into another the most unpleasant and expensive experience of your life.

Some tips for hassle-free border crossings

Having said that, there are some tactics you can employ to make the whole experience a little less horriffic. For example:

o   **Cross using public transport:** That way when the guard starts hassling you he'll have a bus load of impatient locals to deal with as well.

163

- o **Act dumb:** Pretend you don't understand even if the guy is fluent in your native language. After half an hour of charades and your non-comprehending looks, the guy will do one of two things—wave you through in an agitated manner or beat you to within an inch of your life.

- o **Divest yourself of all money and assets:** If you don't have any money or anything of value there's nothing they can take, is there? Of course, this is only apt when leaving a country. Most countries like to see that you have some way of supporting yourself before letting you in.

- o **Observe opening hours:** Borders, like banks, have times when they are open and times when they are closed. You'll find it a lot easier to cross a border when it is actually open.

To bribe or not to bribe, that is the question

In many countries bribes, or *baksheesh,* are a normal and accepted way of getting things done. A little lucre at the right moment can open doors—even borders—when all seems lost.

In all my travels I have never had to bribe my way across a border. I've found that a little patience can get you just as far as a little legal tender. If you're prepared to sit on a border for a couple of hours, a couple of days or even a couple of weeks, I guarantee that you'll be able to get across most borders without having to pay a single cent in bribes. In fact, depending on how aggravating your presence is, they could actually end up paying you to go away.

The power of paperwork

One of the most effective ways of ensuring that the whole border crossing thing goes as smoothly as possible is to have all your paperwork in order. It's amazing how much better things go if you actually go to the trouble of getting a valid passport and the appropriate visa.

164

Of course, any other official-looking piece of paper you can get your hands on helps too. Even if it is in a language they can't understand, border officials the world over are always impressed by a well-designed letterhead.

University letterheads are good for this, as are those of large corporations. If you can get it stamped with an official seal, so much the better.

Don't overlook any paperwork you may be able to pick up while you're travelling too. When a border guard in the Congo insisted on a US$20 'departure tax' I refused to pay him and instead pulled out a photographic permit I picked up in Brazzaville signed by the Minister of Tourism himself. I lied and said that the Minister told me I was exempt from any departure costs. Not only did I avoid the fee, the border guard smoothed the way with the Gabonese border guard, waved down a truck and insisted that it take me to the first town in Gabon for free.

Which borders are the easiest to cross?

Funnily enough, it's the little tin-pot countries in Africa or Asia that often prove the easiest to traverse. In some of those countries, if you either wait long enough or pay enough you'll get across sooner or later. From what I can figure, they don't really care who they let into the country because they know that once you're in and you've sampled their lifestyle, you're not going to want to stay any longer than you have to.

Which are the most difficult?

In my experience, it's the supposed 'civilised' countries like the United States, Australia and those in Western Europe that prove the most difficult.

Each of these countries seem to employ the same kind of individuals to guard their borders—pale, acned souls who love bureaucracy and revel in its arcane ability to cause pain and suffering. Visit those countries and, believe me, your visa better be in order. These guys will not hesitate to put you on the first plane back out, usually with the most expensive airline available.

165   Even when everything is in order, they'll try to hassle you. Every time I enter the UK I get grilled for half an hour about my financial, sexual and political leanings before they grudgingly give me the six-month tourist visa I'm entitled to. The US officials insisted that I should have got my visa before I left home, even though that had been a year previously and I'd had a new passport issued since. Give me a drunken African guard after a $10 bribe plus my Swiss army knife any day.

The two sides of border crossings

A lot of people tend to forget that there are two parts to every successful border crossing: leaving one country and then entering another. What's more, both demand very different, very specific skills.

How to leave a country

You may think that leaving a country is a relatively easy process. Having spent time and money in a country, you might be tempted to think that the officials manning the border will politely thank you for propping up their troubled economy and send you on your way.

Not on your life. It is the express purpose of immigration and customs officials processing your departure to relieve you of any money that you may have failed to spend in their miserable country. What's more, the tricky bastards will attempt to do it in one of three ways.

The subtle way

The opening gambit for the subtle approach is 'Do you have a souvenir for me?'.

The best thing to do when asked this question is to pull out some horrendous wood carving that you bought while you were drunk and offer them this. Now, to you, it might be the buy of your trip. But to the average border official it is a worthless piece of junk, pretty much in the manner that a snow dome with a plastic representation of your home town is to you. Chances are the guard will refuse your offer and wave you through just as you start offering him the soapstone elephant.

The legalistic way

This is where the border guard will find some reason to hassle you and charge you an extra fee. The most common reason is an alleged discrepancy with your passport, your visa or your currency declaration form. At other times, they may claim they are about to close up and go home for the day even if it is only 10 am.

If there is something actually wrong with your paperwork, I'm afraid you're going to have to pay up. But take heart from the fact that you can haggle over the amount. Border officials are as open to the idea of bargaining as the fellow who sold you a carpet or a wood carving. In fact, they'll be disappointed if you don't.

The brutal way

The brutal approach is direct and more difficult to overcome. It is a straight demand for money that is sometimes backed up by some sort of firepower or sharp object. The best way to handle this is to cough up the cash, although an equally brutal and direct refusal can sometimes work.

How to enter a country

In order to make the process of entering another country easy, you need to understand one thing about the mindset of immigration and customs officials. No matter how flyblown, sad or pathetic their country, and no matter how pristine and correct your passport and visa, they are convinced that they are doing you an immense favour by letting you in. Things will go a lot smoother if you act suitably thankful.

A prime example is when I went to Burundi with a couple of mates. We strolled in during the midst of a massacre as most people were clambering to get out on the last available Air France jumbo. Two of us got through the border formalities easily enough, but our good mate Sean was being hassled because of a small rust stain on his passport photo. Sean defended himself quite eloquently and his point about the relevance of this guy questioning his identity photo during a mass evacuation was particularly well made. But it wasn't until he said 'please' that the guy finally let him in.

Having said that, my travels have shown that there are three main ways of entering a country.

The straightforward approach

Your paperwork is in order and the border guard is in a good mood. He stamps your passport quickly and neatly, and sends you on to the customs official who, in a similarly good mood, waves you through with a smile.

167

There are no written records of this ever happening.

The lengthy approach

You arrive at a border to find every man and his goat trying to cross at the same time. Although there are a number of booths, only two or three are actually manned. When you finally reach your booth the immigration official closes the booth and goes to lunch. You join another queue and the same thing happens. On reaching the customs official, your bag will be emptied and thoroughly rifled through. On finding nothing, the surly customs official will wave you through and then berate you for taking so long to repack your bag.

This should be considered normal.

The 'I wish I was never born' approach

You will arrive in a country to find that an overnight diplomatic incident means that you need a visa or, worse, the visa will now cost three times as much. The immigration official will either refuse to let you in or insist that the visa be paid for in a currency you have never heard of. He will kindly offer to exchange money for the transaction at a rate that is nothing short of criminal.

168

Having barely survived the immigration process, you find a sniffer dog chewing on your pack and a corpulent customs official smiling at you viciously. When a search of your pack fails to reveal any illicit substances, the rubber gloves are called for and you are ritually humiliated. You finally leave the border with a slight limp and a determination to catch the first flight home.

Increasingly common, particularly in EU countries.

How should I look when I cross a border?

Once again there are two sides to this story. At the immigration post of the country you are leaving it is best that you look as dishevelled and destitute as possible in order to discourage the asking of bribes. However, when entering the next country, it is better that you look neat, tidy and able to support yourself and not just a drug habit.

This need not be a problem. At many border crossings there is quite a distance between the border posts of two countries, allowing you ample time to get changed, slap on a little deodorant and slick back your hair. The fact that rivers mark the border between some countries means that you can often have a quick wash as well.

Tell me about 'no-man's-land'

No-man's-land is the strip of land between the border posts of one country and another. In some places, like the border between North and South Korea for example, it is literally a no-man's-land, with anyone seen there being shot. Yet in others, it would be more appropriately described as 'everybody's-land'.

Take the border crossing between Kenya and Tanzania at Isebania, for example. The road between the two borders is lined with shops, hotels, bars and restaurants with people going about their business, buying and selling in a variety of currencies. In a small field up near the Tanzanian post, you'll find the world's largest plastic shoe bazaar, with hundreds of thousands of shoes of different colours, sizes and styles laid out on tattered blankets for you to peruse before heading into your next country. If you need a drink or you forgot to change some money on the black market, the border guards are willing to oblige by letting you back into no-man's-land after they have stamped you in.

Should I use a remote border crossing?

Remote border crossings have a lot going for them. There are less crowds, the opening hours are more flexible and, chances are, the immigration official hasn't heard about the expensive new visa regulations.

There are drawbacks, however. Because the crossing is very rarely used, the immigration official will often use all his spare time to pursue other business interests. It could take you days, even weeks, to track him down to stamp you in. Similarly, while he may not have heard of expensive new regulations way out at his isolated outpost, he also may not have heard that his country's visas are now free as well.

169

Worse, he may have run out of currency declaration forms. And do you think that the border official on the other side of the country is going to believe that one when you're trying to leave a couple of months later?

Finally, there are usually very good reasons why a border crossing is rarely used. These include lack of public transport or even roads, lack of villages, people, food and the fact that the surrounding area is a God-forsaken shithole.

What about border tensions?

Travelling some of the more volatile regions of the world, you may come across the problem of a border being closed because of some sort of misunderstanding or border raid. It is nothing a little of the green stuff can't fix.

If you have been travelling for a while, you may come across another kind of border tension—one within your travelling group. During a particularly tricky crossing between Tanzania and Rwanda, I had a falling out with a travelling companion who accused me of suffering from the three worst social diseases: conceit, arrogance and intolerance. A bit rich, I think, from someone who went on to get herpes, a more socially shackling disease by anyone's standards.

170

TOP 10 CHALLENGING BORDER POSTS

What is it that makes a border crossing challenging? Is it the mind-numbing agony of pitting your wits against some petty bureaucrat? Is it the physical rigours of unpacking and packing your bag for a motley assortment of immigration and customs officials? Or is it the stupor inducing stress of trying to cross without shelling out a bribe? If the truth be known, it's all these things—and more, like in the 10 examples below.

1. Congo/Gabon

Once I had convinced the Congolese border guard that I wasn't going to pay his dubious US$20 'departure tax', the most challenging part of this border crossing was trying not to pass out drunk before a logging truck came along to take me to the first town in Gabon. Impressed by my refusal to cough up the cash, the guard spent the entire morning and most of the afternoon plying me with beer brought to us by a small boy from a hut set on a hill just over in Gabon. Just as he was offering me the hindquarter of the rat he had just cooked on a small charcoal fire, a truck arrived. My new-found friend considered it bad luck. I was convinced it was divine intervention.

2. China/Laos

Armed with a transit visa that only allowed me to fly into Laos, I didn't fancy my chances getting across on foot. Nor was I hopeful when I found out that the border was closed to 'third class' countries—and that China regarded Australia as 'third class'.

If there's one thing that impresses the Chinese, however, it's stoic patience. And my three-hour stint at the border, sitting peacefully on the vinyl couch and smiling mindlessly, impressed them no end. But if I had to be really honest though, I think it was my tragic tale about how my father died in a plane accident that finally won them over. With the appalling record of the national Chinese airline (in 1992 it accounted for one-fifth of the world's air passenger fatalities), it's something most Chinese can relate to.

3. Colombia/Ecuador

My guidebook described San Miguel, the last town on the Colombian side of the river that divides Colombia and Ecuador, as 'more a sordid collection of brothels and honky-tonk bars than a town'.

And so it was. But it wasn't what made this border crossing a challenging one. It was the clowns who owned the boats taking passengers to the other side of the river and into Ecuador. Being a quiet day, they figured it would be fun to change which boat was going first and have me jump from one boat to another. They even took to using a megaphone to instruct me. When I finally refused to move from one boat and other passengers began to join me, they soon lost interest and actually cast off our boat and headed for Ecuador.

4. Uganda/Zaire

This was a lesson in the swings and roundabouts of crossing borders. Before stamping my visa, the rather shifty Zairian border guard on duty that day enquired whether I would like to change any money. Considering this was one of the most notorious border crossings throughout Africa, with constant reports of rape and theft, I decided not to upset him and changed $10. He promptly stamped my passport, waived the customs search and stopped a truck to take me to Beni. Even though the rates he offered were a good 75 per cent less than the official rates, I think I got off pretty lightly.

172

5. Turkey/Iran

Imagine, if you can, thousands of overdressed Islamic men and women in a cramped airless room pounding on a metal door demanding to be let into Iran. Well, that's the sight that confronted me on a day when the mercury was pushing 40˚C. Periodically, a guard slid open a peephole, indicating with his eyes who could come through, and then opening the door to let those lucky few in. Any ideas the rest of us had about storming through with the chosen few were quickly dispelled by the sight of four well-armed guards pointing their guns at us. What made the whole process really memorable, however, was being watched by a painting of the Ayatollah, looking down upon us with that particular smirk of his.

6.   Pakistan/Afghanistan

When I arrived at this border crossing at Torkham at the end of the Khyber Pass, it was closed for lunch. One of the friendly locals suggested I try the 'other' border crossing a few hundred metres away. I followed him along a dry riverbed until we came to a sandy road, cut through the low rocky hills. The road was used by 'entrepreneurs' smuggling tax-free western goods from Afghanistan into Pakistan on the backs of camels. Needless to say these 'entrepreneurs' were not impressed by my presence and promptly sent me back to the 'proper' crossing. Still the sight of those camels plodding along the sandy path piled high with 54 cm-screen Sonys is one that will always stay with me.

7.   Burundi/Tanzania

Perhaps one of the most eventful border crossings I've ever made. It started with a massacre in Bujumbura, continued with a friend nearly being shot for tossing a rotten avocado at the feet of a particularly pissed-off Tutsi soldier, and ended with a three-kilometre walk through some of the most breathtaking scenery I'd seen in Africa. As border crossings go, I guess you could say it had it all.

8.   Nepal/Tibet

It is a little known fact that the Himalayas make their most spectacular and rapid ascent between the Nepalese border post in Kodari and the corresponding Chinese border post in Zhangmu.

Rather than stay the night in Kodari and catch a truck up to Tibet the next morning, I foolishly thought I could ascend the eight kilometres to the Chinese border before it closed at 4 pm. The road wound up the side of the mountain in such exaggerated loops that kilometres could

173

be cut off by using the near vertical paths that dissected them. What I didn't realise was that these same paths also cut off a will to live. I staggered into Zhangmu at 8 pm ready to end it all and had my passport confiscated for good measure.

9. Tanzania/Rwanda

I have met some surly and petty border officials in my time but none of them come close to the jumped-up bureaucrat controlling the Rwandan border post at Chutes de Rusumo. Convinced that he had the power of the Rwandan President himself—conferred of course—this man set about interrogating us with Nazi efficiency. Who were we? Where were we from? What were our intentions in Rwanda? It was only when he reached for his stamp pad to finally let us in that I realised why. On his desk—and this is no word of a lie—was a biography of Adolf Hitler. He'd obviously liked what he read.

10. Kenya/Somalia

The Kenyan army officers guarding the lonely border post at Kiunga wouldn't let me cross into Somalia unless I left all my valuables with them at the border. They claimed that the Somali Shifta bandits would kill me if they thought I had anything worth stealing. I suspected that they would sell it all the moment I got beyond the first rise. Unfortunately, if I wanted to get into Somalia—and who doesn't?— I would have to trust them.

As it turned out, I could. I returned a week later and found all my belongings intact. I must admit, however, that I was disturbed by the fact that they seemed genuinely surprised to see me.

174

SEX & ROMANCE

Forget your oysters and ground-up rhino horns. It's travel that is the greatest aphrodisiac known to man. Balmy nights, romantic vistas, randy backpackers—it's a heady mix that makes making out downright irresistible.

I can't find a lover at home. How is travelling going to be any different?

The ground rules are different when you're travelling. Whereas you will be treated as a loony if you start up a conversation with the person sitting next to you on the train back home, you will be swamped with gratitude if you try the same thing when you're travelling.

Nor do you have to worry about being witty and erudite. To a person who hasn't heard English for a couple of weeks anything you say will sound interesting.

And if you're no oil painting, don't worry either. It's amazing how handsome the geekiest guy will look to a girl who has just spent 12 hours on a bus being molested by oversexed hill tribesmen.

What pick-up lines work best when travelling?

The secret is to be sincere and unaffected. Travellers can smell a sleaze a mile off—especially if they haven't washed for a couple of weeks.

If you must use a line, here are some that I have heard work:

175

176

Of course, other more imaginative lines can work too. A friend of mine swept a young American doctor off her feet by asking her about the problem of topsoil degradation in the United States. Another friend bedded a college girl by having a good working knowledge of the writings of Thomas Hardy. A handy hint, guys: it's the lesser works like 'A Pair of Blue Eyes' that impress.

What are my chances with the locals?

If you are a guy, not very good. For one thing, you probably won't be staying long enough to strike up a meaningful relationship with that attractive French brunette sitting opposite you on the Metro. And let's be realistic, why would she want to have anything to do with an unwashed, unshaved Neanderthal like you anyway?

If you are a girl, however, the odds are excellent. No matter how unattractive you may be feeling after a 48-hour train ride, the gaggle of would-be Romeos waiting just outside the station will think you are the most beautiful woman this side of Liz Hurley. The poorer the country, the more attractive you will appear.

I've heard that in some countries the women throw themselves at you

That's true. They're called prostitutes. They cost money and they can give you more than you bargained for.

Am I going to meet the love of my life travelling?

Of course you are. It's inevitable that you will meet someone attractive, charming, witty and sexy, and who thinks you are too.

Unfortunately, it is also inevitable that you will meet them an hour or two before your flight back home and that you will never see them again.

Can I turn a holiday romance into a fulfilling lifetime relationship?

Unfortunately, no. The cool long-haired guy you met at the Full Moon party at Ko Pha-Ngan will inevitably turn out to be an aggressive investment banker who will spend more time worrying about his career and stock portfolio than about you when you catch up six months later.

Similarly, the blissed-out babe who showed you the meaning of true enlightenment at an ashram in India will turn out to be a power-dressing bitch, too ashamed to introduce you to her corporate buddies.

Of course, some people are the same at home as they are travelling. But they tend to be the people that are always getting lost and getting mugged.

177

In short, holiday romances should be treated as what they are: a chance for ordinary people to let down their hair and have a good, old fashioned, no-strings-attached shag.

If I do get lucky, should I use condoms?

Travelling is about experiencing new cultures and fostering goodwill amongst humankind. In short, you are an ambassador for your country. It wouldn't be very nice to go infecting total strangers with your afflictions, would it?

If you're still not convinced, here's a cautionary tale. A friend of mine caught herpes from a Canadian girl in Africa. The upshot of it all is that he can't eat sesame seeds anymore.

Should I take condoms with me?

Whether you are a guy or girl, going to the trouble of taking condoms when travelling is the surest way of ensuring that you won't get laid. Similarly, the surest way to get lucky is to be caught out condom-less with no way in sight of getting hold of any.

It is far better to buy them as you need them. Just imagine the joy of breaking from an amorous clinch to wander the streets of a foreign city trying to find a chemist that is not only open, but can understand what it is you want to buy.

• •
An important tip: Should you have to resort to charades to make yourself understood when buying condoms, try not to make them too explicit. You can get arrested for that sort of thing in some countries.
• •

What is the mile-high club and how do I join it?

The 'mile-high club' is a club where the only rule of admission is that you have to fornicate while at least a mile above the earth's surface—usually in an aeroplane. While some charter companies offer plane services especially, most people join on a normal commercial flight.

178

Joining the mile-high club with the Scandinavian temptress who just happens to be sitting next to you on a long flight ranks second only to having an affair with a local girl as the most popular male travel fantasy. Travellers should realise that this is all it is—a fantasy. Anyone who has flown any distance knows that it's much more likely that you will be sitting next to a Sumo wrestler than a blonde, blue-eyed babe.

Couldn't I join with my boyfriend/girlfriend?

To be honest, this is your best chance. Having someone you are intimate with does away with the need of: (a) getting a seat beside an oversexed Swede in the first place; and (b) convincing the said Swede that he/she should whip off to the toilet with a smelly backpacker like you for a good rogering.

It should be noted that even then, joining the mile-high club is still fraught with dangers. A friend of mine made an attempt on a flight to Rome. He and his girlfriend slipped past the air hostess and squeezed into the toilet cubicle somewhere over southern France. After tearing each other's clothes off, he suffered temporary performance anxiety. The thought of an angry stewardess pounding on the door rendered him temporarily impotent.

Where is the best place for me to consummate my holiday romance?

The beauty of travel is that you are freed of the normal constraints of the four walls of your bedroom or the back seat of your car. Should the mood strike you, you could take your new found beau to the Savoy in London or a quaint little pensione overlooking the Adriatic in Italy.

Of course, natural and man-made wonders also offer a host of possibilities. Who amongst us hasn't contemplated doing it on a raft thundering down Victoria Falls or on top of the Pyramids?

It should be noted, however, that not all countries will share your enlightened views about sex on public monuments.

TOP 10
FANTASY
LOCATIONS

When you're travelling, where you consummate your holiday romance can be more important than who you do it with. Here are some suggestions for places that could make the whole experience unforgettable—or end up landing you in jail.

1. Anywhere in Budapest

On the subway, in the parks, at the Fisherman's Bastion, even in the grounds of the Albanian Embassy—one can't turn around on the streets of Budapest without coming across a couple in an amorous clinch. Freed from the stifling constraints of communism, everyone is at it hammer and tongs in 'Bonking Budapest'. Why shouldn't you be?

2. The 337 to Richmond via Putney, London

The 337 is one of those quaint, red double-decker buses. Late at night, chances are you'll have the whole top floor to yourself. The trouble is that these buses now have hidden surveillance cameras so your antics are likely to be taped and swapped around other bus drivers. Moreover, they could also end up on a black market soft porn video called 'On the Buses'.

3. Mount Sinai, Egypt

High amongst the jagged mountains of the Sinai desert, this is the spot where Moses got the Ten Commandments. Bloody cold, and bordering on the sacrilegious, it's the amazing amount of shooting stars at night that make it an unforgettable venue.

179

4. A pensione in Florence, overlooking Piazza Signoria

A Florentine pensione is the perfect place to live out your *Room with a View* fantasies. Guys get to think they're Julian Sands. Girls can pretend they're Helena Bonham Carter. And owners of cramped, decrepit garrets get to make lots of money.

5. The Tor, Glastonbury

Set on a hill amongst the lush green patchwork of fields in southern England, the Tor could be the last resting place of King Arthur. It's also a magnet for every crusty, spiritualist and new age traveller this side of India. Your attempts to recreate the grand passion of Lancelot and Guinevere are likely to be interrupted by a New Zealand healer trying to recharge her crystals.

6. Cheops Pyramid, Egypt

An amazing spot where you'll have 4000 years of history beneath you. Trouble is, it will take you all night to scramble up the huge sandstone blocks to the top. Chances are that you'll be too tired to do anything when you get there.

7. Stone Forest, Kunming, China

A massive collection of grey limestone pillars with very phallic overtones. I'm not sure that anyone has actually done it here, as the guy who told me about it thought I had asked him about the most amazing place he has ever 'slept'. Still, by the way he described the moon shining on the phallic formations at night, it sounds as though it could be interesting.

180

8. A felucca on the Nile

Could anything be more romantic than floating down one of the world's great rivers in a sailboat that has changed little in design since the days of the Pharaohs? I should point out that there are problems to overcome first. You could be too stoned to do anything or you may be put off by the felucca captain drooling and leering and trying to get in on the action himself.

9. A tropical island in the Maldives

Sugar-white beaches. Aqua blue water. Quaint reed huts set amongst palm trees that whisper as the wind rustles through them at night. No wonder the Maldives is one of the most popular honeymoon destinations in the world. A little known fact, however, is that many marriages go unconsummated because of third-degree sunburn.

10. A 'free love' ashram in India

Anyone who spends any time in India will hear of an ashram where, after an AIDS test, you are allowed to sleep with everyone and anyone you choose. It sounds great, but if you press the person telling you about it for more details, all you'll get is that it's somewhere in southern India and that it was a friend of theirs who went there, not them.

Chapter 19

SOUVENIRS

They're an integral part of the travel experience—the memories or mementoes we bring back as reminders of our journeys. Sometimes we buy them, sometimes they're given to us and sometimes we're not even aware that we have them. They're souvenirs, and this is everything you need to know about them.

How will I know a souvenir when I see one?

It's quite easy. Just ask yourself these questions:

o   Is it tacky and impractical?

o   Is it overpriced?

o   Is it made of plastic or some other dubious man-made substance?

o   Does it lack any inherent craftsmanship or quality?

o   Does it fail utterly to reflect the culture of the country it is being sold in?

o   Are there numerous stalls nearby selling the exact same item?

o   Does the shop also sell film, postcards and Coca-Cola?

o   Will I immediately regret buying it?

If you answer yes to one or more of these questions, congratulations! You have found a souvenir.

Are there other types of souvenirs?

183

Of course. By definition, a souvenir is something that brings back memories of a place you have visited. It could be a gift given to you by a friendly local. It could be the wad of local currency that the bank back home refuses to touch. It could even be the photos you took that didn't quite turn out the way you had hoped.

It can also be a 'memento' that you didn't realise you'd picked up—like a nasty disease, for example. This can define your memories of a particular country as vividly as a wooden mask or a soapstone elephant.

What makes a good souvenir?

Good souvenirs capture the essence of a particular country. A popular souvenir from Singapore, for example, is the receipt for your $500 fine for forgetting to flush the toilet. From New York, it's the police report from when you were mugged. From Australia, it's the stuffed toy koala that was actually made in China. Whatever it is, a good souvenir is as individual as your own travel experiences.

What sort of things shouldn't I buy?

I'm not about to get entangled in a debate about what makes a good souvenir and what doesn't. After all, one man's trash is another's treasure. And as an avid collector of plastic snow domes, I don't feel that my credibility is too high in this area anyway.

Having said that, there are some other rather less arbitrary rules that should be taken into account when you're buying your stash of mementoes. For one thing, there's no use spending good money on an item only to have it confiscated by the folks in customs when you get home. Best to leave that turtle-shell guitar on the shelf!

Similarly it's no good picking up a kilo of hash—no matter how much of a bargain it is—if some sniffer dog is going to find it and you end up in jail.

Finally, think twice before you go buying all that 'ethnic' clothing. Sure, it looks cool while you're travelling and if that's all you're buying it for, go right ahead. But please reconsider your purchase if you're under the serious misapprehension that you are going to wear it when you get back home. As someone with a wardrobe full of the stuff—and a job where I could possibly even wear it without getting sacked—let me tell you that you won't.

184

How should I buy a souvenir?

Always bargain from the perspective that what you're buying is an absolute worthless piece of crap—99.9 per cent of the time this is indeed the case.

If it's not the case, and the carved statue you bought from the camel boy at the pyramid really turns out to be Pharaonic, well, you've come out ahead haven't you? At least until you get busted at Cairo airport for trying to smuggle out antiquities.

Can souvenirs be investments?

Yeah, right! When was the last time you saw Sotheby's auction off a collection of souvenir tea towels or plastic snow domes?

Seriously, though, you will come across individuals in your travels who will try to sell you all kinds of things as 'investments'. Carpet sellers in Istanbul, gem dealers in Bangkok, Cockney spruikers in $2 shops in Australia—they'll all beguile you with wonderful tales of people who made 100, 200 even 1000 per cent profit by selling these items when they got home. The truth of the matter is that most of those travellers probably were either ripped off severely or ended up in jail.

I fell victim to this ploy myself. I swapped a pen for what I thought was a ruby with some lads in an abandoned pagoda in Pagan, Burma. When I took it to a jeweller back home I found out it was a piece of red-coloured glass. But that's all right. They thought they were getting a gold pen. In reality, it wasn't even gold-plated. It was just gold-coloured.

What if I'm offered 'local prices'?

A common ploy used by many shopkeepers is to tell a swaying buyer that he is offering the said item to them at 'local prices'. The inference is that the local price is much lower than the tourist price. But ask yourself, what kind of local is going to buy a brightly-painted wooden mask when he has an extended family to feed? That's right—a mad one who has no idea of the value of money. It's a sobering thought, isn't it?

185

The NSITT glossary of other dubious souvenir terms

Authentic: Created in a sweatshop in southern China to authentic designs lifted from an encyclopaedia.

Antique: Made yesterday for people born yesterday.

Genuine: You are being genuinely ripped off.

Hand Made: A human hand was involved somewhere in the production of the particular item, probably at the very beginning to turn on the machine.

186

Should I wait until the end of my trip to buy souvenirs?

Numerous disappointments over the years have taught me to buy a souvenir I like the moment I clap eyes on it. Although I may be tempted by all manner of sensible reasons as to why I shouldn't buy it straight away—like lack of funds, for example—experience has taught me to ignore them.

Even if you are returning to the same place at the end of the trip, it is inevitable that you will find that the said souvenir will be gone. Similarly, if you think you'll be able to buy it somewhere else, you'll find that it is more expensive and of a poorer quality.

Should I buy a souvenir from the person who made it?

Many travellers foolishly think that souvenirs are cheaper and better quality when they are bought from the place where they are made. That's why there are so many towns and villages around the world that tout themselves in tourist literature as centres of weaving, wood carving and plastic extrusion expertise.

It's also why so many people end up disappointed and ripped off. They arrive in these 'centres' to find that all the really good stuff has been sent off to souvenir shops and international hotels in the capital city and all that's left are the mistakes and failures. What's more, the artisans charge a fortune for these mistakes knowing that some travellers will pay a heavy premium just to be able to say that they bought it from the person who made it when the item is admired—or ridiculed—at their next dinner party.

Should I post souvenirs home?

If you are really hard-pressed for space or have been on a totally uncontrolled souvenir-buying rampage, you could contemplate sending your souvenirs home by post. And why not? It certainly adds to the excitement of your journey.

Firstly, you'll get to experience the mind-numbing bureaucracy that is the parcel division of any post office in the world. Secondly, you'll enjoy the adrenaline rush of handing over items of value without quite knowing whether you'll ever see them again. And thirdly, you'll witness the torpor of your pathetic 9 to 5 existence being temporarily lifted when a note from the post office arrives to let you know that the parcel you sent has finally arrived.

In that way sending your souvenirs back by post is like Christmas— except, of course, you already know what the present is supposed to be. The element of surprise comes in finding out what your country's customs officials have decided to confiscate.

It's not just your country's customs officials you've got to watch either. I once sent a package back from Sri Lanka that included a pair of Nikes I had bought cheaply in Singapore. Before I could send the package it had to be inspected by a customs official at Colombo post office, just to ensure that I wasn't sending back a kilo or two of Semtex as well. The lascivious way he eyed my new runners made me think I would never see them again. Three months later the parcel arrived, and to my surprise the runners were still there. I was lucky. I can only surmise that they didn't fit the guy—or anyone else in the Sri Lankan postal service.

Can souvenirs liven up a journey?

Certainly. An injudiciously purchased souvenir, particularly an extremely fragile or large one, can add unexpected dimensions to your journey. Like the toy helicopter I bought on my first night in Vietnam, for instance.

It was made from aluminium cans and was totally unsuited for the long and treacherous journey to Hanoi I was about to undertake. But in my inebriated state, I didn't think about that.

187

I was just impressed at the ingenuity of its maker and the fact that it only cost a dollar. When I woke up the next morning I named it 'Apache One' after the helicopter in the battle scene in John Woo's *A Bullet in the Head* and set myself the task of carrying it from one end of Vietnam to the other.

For three weeks I carefully cradled it on a variety of buses, vans and trains and each night hung it up in the bathroom of my room. I take great pride in the fact that Apache One survived the journey intact, except for a slightly bent rear rotor, and now has pride of place on my bookshelf. But then, I'm strange like that.

Does buying a souvenir help the local economy?

188

My word! With the ludicrous mark-up on most souvenirs, especially the big ticket items like carpets and jewellery, each of your purchases takes a sizeable chunk off the current account deficit of the particular country you are visiting.

The notable exception to this is Australia. All the souvenirs in Australia, right down to the tiniest of cling-on koalas, have been produced overseas. Rather than help Australia's rather dire economic circumstances, the proceeds of your purchase will immediately wing its way to the booming People's Republic of China.

Tell me about pirate souvenirs

One of the big growth areas in souvenirs—especially in China and other parts of South East Asia—are pirate souvenirs. These souvenirs are crudely copied versions of sought-after Western goods that sell for a mere fraction of the cost of the original. A backpacker combing the back-streets of Hanoi is now more likely to come away with the latest Oasis CD than one of those funny conical hats. Similarly, in Istanbul it's harder to resist the temptation of 10 pairs of Lacoste socks for $1 than that of a genuine Turkish carpet for $300.

Of course, buying a pirated good has its drawbacks. The quality is never going to be as good. And in the case of pirated CDs, the artwork is usually only ever cursory. Not that that's a problem. With lyrics like 'Slowly walking down the hall, faster than a cannon ball', it's probably for the best that you don't get the lyric sheet with *(What's the Story?) Morning Glory*.

What's this about *giving* souvenirs?

When you visit some of the less fortunate countries, rather than buy souvenirs, you will be expected to give them. In fact, in some countries 'Do you have a souvenir for me?' is the only English phrase the locals know.

Their definition of 'souvenir' may be a little different to what you are used to as well. To these individuals 'souvenir' covers your camera, clothes, Walkman and any cash you may be carrying at the time. Once, when I was frisked at a roadblock in Colombia, a soldier asked for the Swiss army knife he found in my pocket as a souvenir. Although he was carrying a loaded gun at the time he seemed to take my curt 'No' fairly well.

To avoid such confrontations, you might want to take along some small worthless gifts to give away. Cigarettes or something representative of your country always go down well. I always take a packet of little cling-on koalas with me. Not only do they get me out of my immediate predicament, they are also crappy enough to discourage the recipient from ever asking a traveller for a souvenir again.

TOP 10 UNUSUAL MOMENTOES

Some people collect wood carvings. Others collect spoons. Some collect those funny little plastic snow domes. But no matter who they are or what they hoard, all they are really collecting is memories. Below you'll find 10 strange items that bring the memories flooding back for me—whether I want them to or not.

1.　A one-Zairee coin

When the bank in Bumba inexplicably gave me this coin as part of the barrow load of money I got when I changed some money in Zaire the going rate was 100,000 Zairees to the US dollar. Less than a year later the exchange rate was closer to 8 million Zairees. That was back in 1992, so imagine how bloody worthless the thing is now. Perhaps that's why I find it so endearing, and keep it tucked away in my wallet. It acts as a reminder that, no matter how low the Aussie dollar sinks, there are other currencies worse off.

190

2.　Tile from the refurbished equator monument, Pontianak

A while ago I had this crazy idea of travelling the world visiting equatorial monuments and this monstrosity on the north bank of the Kapuas River at Pontianak in Kalimantan, Indonesia, was the first significant one I visited.

Unfortunately it was being renovated at the time and the proposed T-shirt/cold drink shop was still under construction. Sensing my disappointment, one of the workmen kindly offered me an offcut from one of the tiles they were laying on the floor as a souvenir. For some inexplicable reason I kept it.

3. Coca-Cola, bottled in Afghanistan

A guy I went with into Afghanistan, risked life and limb to smuggle out a Coca-Cola bottle with 'Bottled in Afghanistan' proudly stamped just below the neck. He figured it would be a talking point back home when people spotted it sitting on the mantelpiece—something that would effortlessly turn the conversation towards a lengthy tirade beginning with 'When I was in Afghanistan …' I just hope he doesn't try to drink it. Having sampled a few in Afghanistan, I can tell you that although the bottles are authentic, the black stuff inside ain't Coca-Cola. In fact, the taste was more of oil and gunpowder.

4. Empty AK47 magazine, Somalia

Souvenir shops are a little thin on the ground in post-Barre Somalia so I had to make do with this rather rusty magazine clip from an AK47. I found it in the sand beside the road as I walked back into Kenya from Chiamboni. After spending close to a week bashing about with the local warlord in a Toyota ute with a machine gun welded to the roof, it seemed an appropriate reminder of my time there.

5. Bosnian cigarette lighter, Mostar

Since the Croats blew up the medieval bridge and the souvenir shops that surrounded it, finding a memento to bring back from Mostar has become something of a challenge. Just as I was about to give up, one of the local guys I was hanging out with offered me his plastic lighter emblazoned with the Bosnian coat of arms. There was one proviso though. I had to take back the cling-on koala I had given him.

6. Tin-can helicopter, Vietnam

OK, with more and more people visiting Vietnam these days, a scale model of a helicopter made from nothing more than aluminium drink cans probably doesn't qualify as unusual any more. By the time you read this there's probably one in every dorm in every campus across America. But, hey, it still gets my vote for most creative interpretation of recycling.

191

7. Giardiasis, fish & chip shop, Nairobi

I thought I was getting a serve of fish and chips, but I ended getting much, much more— a dose of giardias is what saw me spend more time in Kenyan toilets than game parks. A course of Flagyl seemed to do the trick, although I'm always worried that it may crop up again—a memento of Kenya that just 'keeps on giving'.

8. Blessing block from room, Iran

In every room where I stayed in Iran I found little terracotta blocks embellished with pressed Farsi script hidden in the corners. And every time I found one I would pocket it and take it away with me as a souvenir.

I have always suspected that in doing so I was being blasphemous and half expected a fatwa had been declared on me and I would be bailed up at the bus station as I tried to leave. It never happened. If I ever get one of them translated, I'm sure it will say nothing more than 'Dear Allah, please protect my humble establishment from this smelly backpacker'.

9. 37 Orange Crush bottle tops, Zaire

192

I spent 10 days in Bumba waiting for the barge I was travelling on to continue down the Zaire River. And in that time I drank a lot of the local Orange Crush. Each bottle was topped with a white cap with a smiling orange on it. The orange's happiness was such a sharp contrast to my feelings that I felt compelled to keep the bottle top from each bottle I drank. I ceremoniously lined them up on the wonky table in the concrete cell that was my hotel room and when the barge finally left, I collected them into a small box and brought them home with me.

Now, whenever I'm feeling miserable I drag them out, line them up and remember when I really was miserable. That is until the men in the white coats take them from me.

10. Bark loincloth, Siberut, Indonesia

In Siberut, a small island off the west coast of Sumatra in Indonesia, the locals still gad about in nothing more than a bark loincloth. What's more, they seem to get a great deal of enjoyment out of convincing visiting travellers to do the same.

I must admit, I succumbed, but only after I had been convinced that the loincloth was a genuine one-owner item. Needless to say, I looked ridiculous and have destroyed all photos taken at the time. The bark loincloth is now my only reminder of those days, and it only comes out for weddings, funerals and christenings. And in case you're wondering, yes, it is itchy.

194

Chapter 20

MUSIC

They say that music soothes the savage breast. Any traveller who has spent any time on public transport in the Third World knows it's also quite useful in making a tiresome journey less tiresome or for shutting out the cacophony that accompanies bunking in a hotel room right next to a train station.

But it can be more magical than that. A certain sound or a certain song can mesh perfectly with an event or place and elevate a mundane travel experience into a transcendental one. Then, whenever you hear that song you'll be transported back again—whether you want to be or not.

Is music important?

My word! The right music can add another dimension to your journey. That's why it is absolutely essential that you pack a Walkman, your favourite tapes or discs and as many alkaline batteries as you can carry.

Chuck in a pair of little speakers and you have all you need to create your own party with your fellow travellers or new-found local friends. I remember spending Christmas on the roof of a medieval Arabic house in Lamu in Kenya, listening to Galliano and just chilling out with a group of like-minded travellers. It was one of the highlights of my trip to Africa, and when I listen to that CD now I'm immediately back at the Paradise Guest House, laughing at the manager being arrested for not having a radio licence.

Unfortunately, the ability of music to capture a mood and moment in time also has its drawbacks. Whenever I hear Metallica—which, fortunately, isn't very often—I'm back in a cramped, sweaty bemo in Indonesia with a speaker in one ear and the elbow of a fellow passenger in the other.

Music: some inevitabilities

Don't get me wrong. It's not all heavenly choirs and mystical moments with music. While it can be a highlight of your trip, music can just as easily add a discordant note. Consider the following inevitabilities:

o   You run out of batteries just as you are about to embark on a long, gruesome bus journey.

o   Your seat on the bus is directly under the only speaker on the bus that works. Unable to hear the music, the passengers at the back of the bus convince the driver to turn it up really loud so they can.

o   The music is one of two styles: heavy metal or easy listening. If you're really unlucky it will be a local star's approximation of either—or both.

o   The song you left home to get away from will be just starting to get blanket airplay in the country you are visiting.

o   Your favourite tape is the only tape you bring along. Soon it is no longer your favourite tape.

o   The traveller you've just fallen in lust with has a dreadful habit of singing Whitney Houston songs out loud as you walk along the street.

o   Moments after a beautiful a cappella rendition from a primitive tribe in the backblocks of Indonesia you are asked to return the favour by singing a song from your country. All you can remember is the jingle from a beer commercial.

Are there any problems with taking a Walkman travelling?

The most immediately apparent problem is that it will get stolen and you'll have to buy an inferior Chinese Walkman that is the size of *War and Peace* and sounds as though the headphones are in another room.

However, the biggest problem you'll face is when you pull out your Walkman in a public place. In most places, including some suburbs of Sydney, it will be regarded as a wondrous piece of magic that everyone will want to listen to. You'll spend a couple of hours watching other people nodding their head from side to side in a most unrhythmic fashion and then get nothing but flat batteries and somebody else's ear wax for your troubles.

196

If you're on a bus, and it has a tape player, it's even worse. The bus driver will probably motion to you to bring up the tape so he can play it. You may be tempted into thinking that the bus driver is just being friendly and wants to share your wonderful music with everyone else on the bus. Unfortunately, it's more malicious than that. In reality, it's his way of saying to everyone else on the bus: 'Hey, we might be poor, we might be hungry but at least we don't have to listen to this shit!'. If he's a really nasty individual, he'll play it because he knows his tape player will chew it.

In these situations I find it is best to pretend you don't understand what he is saying.

That's not a problem in a mini-bus full of foreigners though, is it?

I'm afraid so. The tape will probably still get chewed—and this time you'll be able to understand what people are saying about your taste in music.

What about batteries?

Take as many as you can physically carry. Even if you don't use them all you'll be able to secure sexual favours or sell them for a profit to fellow travellers desperate for batteries that will last for longer than one or two songs.

If you are ever placed in the dire situation of having to buy batteries while travelling, a word of warning: don't ever buy a battery that uses an animal as its logo, particularly if the animal is an endangered species. Believe me, even their most endangered namesakes have a longer life expectancy.

What sort of music should I take?

197

There a number of approaches you could take on this one. You could walk into a record store and buy whatever is in the Top Five, hoping that if it's top of the charts at home it's going to be popular with everyone else on the road. Similarly, you might consider taking stuff that makes you appear cool and eclectic. Both approaches could work. Both could clear a room faster than the new Peter Andre single.

It's probably best that you take along music you like. That way at least you'll enjoy yourself. And if everyone groans when you put on your Meatloaf tape, don't worry. I guarantee they'll all be singing along by the time it gets to 'Paradise by the Dashboard Lights'.

You've also got to remember that a lot of the time it's going to be just you and your Walkman. And are you really strong enough to survive a nine-hour bus journey listening to Celine Dion?

Should I swap tapes or discs with other travellers?

If you had a collection of your favourite songs that you really enjoyed listening to, would you want to swap it? Of course you wouldn't. So be very suspicious of people who claim that they do.

I once met this Canadian guy in Turkey who wanted to swap his Bread tape for one of my homemade compilation tapes. When I asked him why he wanted to swap he claimed that it was a tape that had changed his life and now he wanted it to enrich mine. I very nearly fell for it, thinking it mustn't have been the same Bread that I knew. It was, and thankfully, I didn't. The guy later admitted he had fallen for the same con he tried on me in Paris and had been trying to get rid of the tape ever since.

198

What about buying tapes or CDs?

Sure, why not? In places like Bali or Bangkok you'll find a better selection than at home and for a fraction of the cost. The quality can be a bit dodgy but with the advent of cheap CD burners, every man and his dog anywhere from street corners in Istanbul to the London Underground is flogging copies of the latest Radiohead CD the moment it is released. And on Khao San Road and on some of the more touristy islands in Thailand, there is more than one shonky operator making a nice living from backpackers too drunk to notice the difference.

I want to listen to World Music at its source

Since the success of Deep Forest, lots of backpackers have been going to places specifically to seek out ethnic music. More often than not they end up disappointed. Not only are Zairian pygmies unable to afford samplers, they'd rather sit around and listen to Michael Jackson anyway. The ethnic music we're used to hearing is actually made by bored producers in Paris, London or New York.

In fact, anyone with any musical talent in the Third World wants to be in a Western style group anyway. In Asia, they all want to be in heavy metal bands. In Africa, they all want to be rappers.

Once, in a rather squalid market in Loubomo, the Congo—just by the blackened bananas if I remember rightly—I was accosted by a young African guy in a rather loud polyester shirt. Because I was white and had long hair, the lad figured **199** I was a band manager and begged me to take him to America and make him a star. Before I could protest, he started rapping about life on the mean streets of LA. The guy was good, but I declined his offer. He had never been out of the Congo, so I questioned the credibility of his tales of drive-by shootings and 'Homies' and 'Ho's'. Then I finally got to America and realised that credibility didn't matter. I should have signed the guy up.

Will music bring me closer to the locals?

Rather than have you realise what a small world it is, the music of the culture you are visiting will only serve to remind you how different we all are. African music tends to sound like the stuff they play from icecream vans, Chinese music sounds like a cat being strangled and I defy anyone to listen to Italian pop—other than silly Italian teenagers—and feel as though their lives have been enriched by the experience.

Similarly, visitors to Australia and certain pubs in London frequented by Antipodean ex-pats must be perplexed by the enduring popularity of Cold Chisel songs. I was brought up on them and I still am.

Is there any music that sounds better when you're travelling?

Yes. But it's nothing to do with the music. Rather, it's the associations that become attached to it. For example, I usually turn off the radio a few seconds within hearing the first few bars of an Ace of Base song. Yet, thanks to endless nights in bars on the Mediterranean coast of Turkey where it was the only song ever played, I get all misty-eyed and nostalgic when I hear their song 'All That She Wants'. Similarly, whenever I hear 'Everyone's a Winner' by Hot Chocolate I think of a bunch of Swiss hoodlums in cardigans doing donuts on their Vespas as it played on the portable cassette player in a car park overlooking Lake Lucerne.

At other times it's the setting that makes some music more palatable. I've never been a big Sting fan, yet I shelled out US$25 to see him play in the old amphitheatre in Ephesus. The ancient stone seats, the flawless acoustics and the stunning sunset of the broken pillars lining the promenade towards the coast made the whole event unforgettable. I was so overwhelmed that I rushed out and bought a pirate CD of *Ten Summoner's Tales*. I haven't played it since.

What about high culture?

This is a bit more difficult because there are some styles of music that you are never going to warm to, no matter how extravagant or mind-blowing the setting. Buoyed by my experience with Sting, I foolishly decided to go and see an opera in the magnificent opera house in Budapest. It was the first time I had ever been to the opera and I figured that watching it in one of the grandest opera houses in the world would make it an unforgettable experience.

Unfortunately, I was right. On the program that night was a six-hour Wagnerian epic—*Parsifal*, if I remember rightly—in four parts. After two acts shifting uncomfortably in my chair I abandoned the show and went to Morrison's, the English-style pub just around the corner. There I sipped on pints of fine English ale and watched a more palatable tragedy unfold—England being bowled out for 46 by the West Indies after needing only 193 to win.

Tell me about music-oriented destinations

In recent years, a number of Third World entrepreneurs have taken to organising dance parties in order to make their fortune. They stage them in an exotic tropical locale like Goa in India or Ko Pha-Ngan in Thailand, link it to some suitably mystical event like a full moon and sit back and let the rupees or baht roll in. Young people flock in from all over the world, drawn by the romantic notion of ingesting copious amounts of illicit substances, dancing to the pneumatic beat of techno all night long and copulating in the sand. Most end up getting arrested and calling their parents for the money to cover the bribe to get them out of jail.

Are discos around the world different?

Apart from a few little idiosyncrasies—like the currency they accept at the door and the bizarre insistence in Dutch discos that guys with long hair keep it in a ponytail—discos are amazingly similar the world over. They all have silver mirror balls, they all charge ridiculous prices for drinks and they all employ bouncers who are as ugly as they are stupid.

Even the music is surprisingly uniform. Now that MTV reaches nearly every corner of the globe, a hit on the dance floors in London is just as likely to be a hit on the dustier dance floors in Africa.

So if you're not a real disco or nightclub person back home, think twice before going while you're travelling. To paraphrase the Australian band, Weddings, Parties, Anything: if you hate Whitney Houston in Sydney, London or Auckland, what makes you think you're going to like her any better in a disco in Prague?

Should I dance when I'm travelling?

If you're a talented dancer, why not? Good footwork is respected the world over and, who knows, it could be the break you've been looking for with the attractive local you've had your eye on.

If, however, you're the kind of person that has paramedics rushing to your side every time you take to the dance floor think twice. A lot of people who would otherwise steer clear of a dance floor are lulled into giving it a go when they are travelling. Encouraged by alcohol, amorous intentions or the knowledge that they are in a foreign country, a million miles away from home and anyone who knows them, they get up on the dance floor and make a fool of themselves—terrifying the poor locals in the process. What they fail to take into account is the high percentage of people carrying cameras when they're travelling. I've lost track of how much money I've had to spend buying negatives off fellow travellers.

What if I'm forced to dance against my will?

It does happen, particularly if you're male and you're in Africa. A friend of mine was simply crossing the dance floor to go to the toilet in the Night & Day Bar in Malindi, Kenya, when he was set upon by a rather large Kenyan lady. He's still in therapy.

Similarly, I was dragged up on stage by a male belly dancer in Patara, Turkey. After a few pathetic wiggles and a half-hearted thrust of my pelvis I figured I had done my duty as the comic relief for the night and went to leave the stage. I'd barely gone two steps before the dancer grabbed the back of my jeans and shook them violently saying, 'Let yourself go. Let yourself be'. I couldn't and I didn't, and I spent the rest of the evening walking with a slight limp and speaking in a high-pitched voice.

If you find yourself in this sort of situation, all I can advise is try to remain composed—and nick the film out of every camera there.

What about karaoke?

After high-definition televisions and small family cars, karaoke is Japan's biggest export to the rest of the world. You'll find it in the most bizarre corners of the world.

202

For example, I spent some time in Ambon, an island tucked away in the far corners of the Indonesian archipelago. I was set upon by a rather friendly local guy called Sue who insisted on taking me to every karaoke place in town, including the local karaoke restaurant. It had laser discs nailed to the back wall and patrons ordered a song with their meal. The waiter brought the microphone to the table along with their nasi goreng. It may be considered impolite to speak with your mouth full in Indonesia but it's certainly okay to sing.

Unfortunately, karaoke is something you're never going to get away from, so you would be well advised to brush up on a few numbers before you go away. In my time on the road I have done a heart-wrenching version of Kenny Roger's 'Ruby' in London, a raunchy rendition of Elvis's 'Burning Love' in Sydney and various interpretations of 'My Way' in Tokyo, Ambon, Budapest and in a private home in Eşfahăn, Iran. Strangely, I was only ever allowed to do one song.

TOP 10
TRAVELLING
TUNES

What is it about music and travel? Why is it that certain events and places become so intimately enmeshed with certain songs when you're backpacking? To be honest, I don't know why but I'm really glad that they do. Because when I'm feeling a little jaded or trapped in a routine, all I have to do is put on any of the following songs and I'm back on the road, my backpack cutting into my shoulders and a little tout tugging on my shirt that hasn't been washed for a couple of days.

I think I'll go and put them on right now.

1.   'I Walk the Earth': Voice of the Beehive

Soaring harmonies, chunky guitar and irresistibly romantic lyrics. Probably the only song ever written that captures the energy and romance of just grabbing a pack and hitting the road. When a big international TV network finally gets around to asking me to make a travel series, I'm going to insist that this is the theme song.

(From *Let it Bee*, London Records.)

2.   'She': Hoodoo Gurus

'In the valley, in the valley, secret world below ...'

Months before I got anywhere near Nepal I knew that I'd want this song from Australia's retro Hoodoo Gurus on my Walkman when I got there. I wasn't disappointed. A few months later I gazed upon the Himalayas at Nagarkot, entranced by the ethereal, other worldly feeling of the whole experience. I'm sure the song helped.

203

(From *Mars Needs Guitars*, Big Time Records.)

3. 'Knuckle Too Far': James

Starting with a bass line that sounds like a slowly beating heart, this song doesn't build to any great heights. What it does do, however, is capture the gnawing feeling of emptiness you get when you're returning home after a long journey. I listened to it as I gazed into the darkness from a bus window on a long straight road through Australia's Northern Territory. I was heading home after almost a year away and I wasn't really sure what my future held or even if I had one. This song did nothing to reassure me—in fact, it panicked me a little. That's why I love it so much.

(From *Laid*, Phonogram Records.)

4. 'Jambo Bwana': The Kenyan Safari Band

To me—and to anyone else who's heard of it—this song is Kenya. Contrary to popular opinion, it isn't the happy, carefree nature of this tune that endears it to folk. Nor is it the fact that it uses the only two Swahili phrases most people ever remember—*jambo bwana* and *mzuri sana*. No, I'm afraid it's rather more perverse than that. It's because you hear the bloody thing so many times.

(From *This is the Kenyan Safari Band*, produced by some crappy pirate tape outfit on Tom Mboya Street, Nairobi.)

5. 'Here's Where the Story Ends': The Sundays

There's a whimsical side to England that you don't find in many other nations. And with satellite towns encroaching on that green and pleasant land, it's a side that's getting harder to find there as well. Play this song on your Walkman however, and you'll find it immediately.

(From *Reading, Writing and Arithmetic*, Rough Trade.)

6. 'All That She Wants': Ace of Base

Not the world's greatest song, I'll admit. But to me it's synonymous with a happy three months I spent in Turkey in 1993. It seemed you couldn't walk into a bar anywhere along the coast without it blasting out of some crappy speakers hooked up amongst the vine leaves. Now, every time I hear it, I'm immediately dancing on tables in a roof-top bar overlooking the Mediterranean, flirting with pretty English film students. You've gotta love a song for that!

(From their first album—was it *Happy Nation*? Who knows. You've all probably got it somewhere down the back of your CD collection.)

7.   'Kiss, Kiss, Kiss': The Vengaboys

When a sweet Malagasy girl passed me her Walkman on the train from Fianarantsoa to Manakara and asked me to transcribe the lyrics of her favourite Vengaboy song I should have refused. After two hours of listening and rewinding, I am now one of the few people in the world who actually know what the song is about—and thinks of Madagascar when they hear it.

(From *The Platinum Album*, EMI.)

8.   'Kathmandu': Bob Seger and the Silver Bullet Band

205

I defy anyone to walk around the old hippy area of Freak Street just off Basantapur Square and not hum this song to themselves. You just c-c-c-c-can't help yourself. And as long as you can still spot the odd freak amongst the increasing hordes of tourists in designer hiking boots, the mystical power of this song will continue to evoke a period in time when the hidden kingdom was the coolest, most far-out place on earth.

(From some old Bob Seger album everybody's parents seem to have.)

9.   'Girl from Ipanema': Astrud Gilberto

These days, the girls from Ipanema wear little more than a G-string and the only time you're likely to say 'ahhh' is when you take a dip and one of the beach boys surfaces beside you demanding your watch at knife point. But if you put this classic on your Walkman when you're walking in the shadows of the condos along this famous Brazilian beach, you'll immediately be transported back to a time altogether more pure, mysterious and sexy. That is, until one of the roving street kids spots your Walkman and nicks it.

(From *This is Astrud Gilberto*, by one of those easy listening labels.)

10. Insert your favourite song here

Like everything with travel, the songs that immediately transport *you* back to that little pensione overlooking the Adriatic, won't be the same as the one that has my mind flying back to Italy. That's why I want you to insert your favourite song here. In fact, I want you to do more than that. I want you to go and put it on now.

● ●
Honourable mention: 'Believe' by Cher
Her warbling about 'life after love' was a constant companion throughout Central America in 1998. Damn her!
(From *Believe*, WEA.)
● ●

Chapter 21

TROUBLE

I suppose I should get a few things straight. I don't have a death wish. And, contrary to what my mother might tell you, I don't go looking for trouble. Nor am I encouraging people reading this book to go out and put themselves in danger.

There is a school of thought, however, that says that you haven't had a real trip until you've got yourself into strife, that you haven't seen all that a country has to offer if you haven't had a stoush with their particular brand of red tape or justice.

It is in the interests of balanced reporting, therefore, that I offer the following advice.

Why should I get into trouble?

A run in with the local authorities or a minor brouhaha with a shopkeeper can liven up the most boring of holidays. A few weeks in a Turkish jail for some minor drug offence can make it a trip that you'll never forget.

Similarly, seeking out international trouble spots can be equally beneficial. With the exception of the odd UN peace-keeping division or two, you'll get the place pretty much to yourself. And next time you're at a dinner party and some prat is rattling on about his sanitised Amazonian jungle trek, you can let it drop that you spent a couple of weeks with the mujaheddin in Afghanistan or in a shelled apartment block in Mostar. It's the backpacker equivalent of a gold Rolex.

207

How can I get into trouble?

The good thing about trouble is that it is very easy to get into, no matter where you are or who you are. Just follow your natural urges and soon enough you'll have offended local sensibilities or inadvertently broken some law. If you're still having problems, just indulge in these seemingly innocent activities:

o **Take photos:** How are you to know that the rather drab building to the right of a colourful market stall was in fact the headquarters of the country's secret police?

o **Speak the language:** If you're anything like me, you'll pronounce even the most innocuous of phrases in such a way that they'll sound like you're insulting somebody's mother.

o **Accept packages from total strangers:** An oldie, but a goodie. Particularly potent just before boarding a plane out of Bangkok or Pakistan.

o **Accept food from strangers:** The surest way to wake up naked, broke and with a splitting headache.

o **Buy your train ticket from a vending machine:** You'll have a great time explaining to the ticket inspector why you thought the longest journey on the subway system was also the cheapest.

o **Carry two passports:** Thanks to James Bond movies and their ilk, this is considered as proof in many African countries that you are an international spy—at least until they extract a fairly substantial bribe out of you.

o **Drive:** With a good deal of the rest of the world driving on the wrong side of the road, you're guaranteed to forget yourself and sideswipe a passing motorcycle cop. Thankfully, most accept bribes so you don't have to suffer through lengthy court proceedings.

208

o **Flirt:** Especially dangerous in Islamic countries or in front of your current boyfriend or girlfriend.

What about offending the locals?

Offending people abroad is pretty much the same as offending people at home. Topics like sex, politics and religion are a lightning rod for robust disputation the world over.

Thankfully, the world being the weird and wacky place that it is, there's any number of more colourful ways to upset local sensibilities. In Asia, using your left hand to eat the evening meal is enough to insult even the most gracious of hosts. In Iran, you can get into strife for looking at someone's wife. In some parts of Africa, you're in trouble if you don't. And in Paris, your mere presence is enough to upset most Parisians.

Clothing is another biggie. For some reason, religious fanatics seem to get upset at bra-less women in see-through singlet tops bouncing through their mosque or temple at prayer time. There's just no understanding some people, is there?

Are there benefits in visiting trouble spots?

If you're the kind of traveller that likes to get away from it all and be treated as a stranger used to be treated in the old days—that is, with a mixture of hospitality, hostility, fascination and suspicion—visiting trouble spots is the only way to go.

209

After all, mass tourism and affordable air travel haven't left you many other options. And with the growth of eco-tourism, there just isn't a middle of nowhere anymore. You're just as likely to meet your politically correct neighbour in the Baliem Valley in Irian Jaya or on Wenceslas Square in Prague as you are down at the local newsagent.

So in reality, that only leaves one option: trouble spots. The kind of place your average package tourist avoids like the plague. The kind of place your embassy warns you against going to. The kind of place for which getting a visa is an exercise in patience, inventiveness and deceit. And the sad thing is, there is no shortage of them.

Should I plan my itinerary around hot spots?

Why not? If a cafe gets blown up in Cairo, head to Cairo. If a coach overturns on a highway in Nevada, buy yourself a bus pass. Prices will have dropped, security will be tightened and the chances of the same thing happening again are as slight as your chances of winning the lottery. And if they do, imagine the stories you'll be able to tell at your next dinner party.

What if the current batch of trouble spots don't interest me?

Be patient. Human nature being what it is, a new trouble spot more in tune with your tastes is bound to pop up. Who'd have thought 10 years ago that it would be possible to wander around the old city walls of Dubrovnik without seeing another living soul, let alone a pack of German tourists?

When is the best time to visit a trouble spot?

After the worst of the fighting and just before Thomas Cook put the place back on their itineraries. That way you're not putting your life into too much danger and cafe and hotel owners are most keen to secure your dollars—even if it is only to replace the broken windows or fix the hole left in the roof by a mortar attack.

Are State Department reports a good indication of trouble spots?

Not really. Judging by some of the US State Department Warnings I've read in my travels, it doesn't take much to get black-banned by the big boys in Washington. Sometimes all it takes is questioning the nutritional value of a Big Mac.

Where are the easiest places to get into trouble?

210

Surprisingly, it's not the countries torn apart with civil strife or even some of the more lawless nations of Africa. The easiest place in the world to run afoul of the local authorities is in Singapore.

In this tiny island state you can get fined for littering, chewing gum, jaywalking and even forgetting to flush the toilet. Indulge in a bit of graffiti and you'll be whacked across the backside with a dirty big rattan.

Similarly, in the Maldives, it's just as easy to get into trouble, but in affairs of the heart. In order to marry someone, all you have to do is say 'I marry you, I marry you, I marry you'. Thankfully, for impulsive romantics, it's just as easy to get out of trouble. Rather than chew your arm off the next morning, all you have to say is 'I divorce you, I divorce you, I divorce you'.

211

Where is the best place to get into trouble?

Once again, the Maldives comes out on top. They don't have jails, just thousands of tiny atolls. In their culture, the worst punishment you can dish out to an offender is to banish them to a different island from their friends and family.

They apply the same principle to foreigners. One German tourist was found guilty of murder and was banished to a tiny coral-fringed island with palm trees and sugar-white beaches. He married a local girl and started a new family—all in a jail you're more likely to see in tourist literature.

What should I do if I get into trouble?

For less serious offences, I've found that the best approach is to play the dumb foreigner. Plead ignorance, pretend you can't understand the language and basically look as moronic as possible. If you're lucky, the authorities will let you off with a warning or the sort of bribe that's easily covered by a second mortgage.

For more serious offences, get yourself a good lawyer.

Shouldn't I contact my embassy?

It depends what country you are from. If you're from the United States or Europe, it's probably not a bad idea. Your country probably has some sort of economic or military muscle they can flex to help you out. If you're from somewhere like Australia or New Zealand, settle in for a long wait. If you're lucky, they might let the consul visit every now and then to tell you the latest footy scores. But I wouldn't count on it.

212

TOP 10 CLOSE SHAVES

I have to admit, touch wood, that I've never really been in big trouble while I've been travelling. Either I'm not very perceptive or I've been very lucky. But there have been times that got the old adrenaline pumping. Here are 10 of them.

1.   Yani the hairbraider, Bali, Indonesia

Anyone who has been to Bali, particularly Kuta Beach, knows how persistent the girls offering to braid your hair with colourful beads can be— I also discovered how vengeful.

I didn't want my hair braided but, rather than be followed around all day by a particularly persistent girl called Yani, I made an appointment the next day, figuring that with so many tourists around she wouldn't remember. Wrong! She remembered and I spent the rest of my stay in Kuta dodging zinging elastic bands and flying plastic beads.

2.   Spying, Uganda

213

This incident started innocently enough. A friend I was travelling with saw a boy with a head shaped like one of those aerodynamic cycle helmets and took a photo of him. Within seconds she was surrounded by secret police. Apparently the bus station where the boy was selling soft drinks was regarded as a politically sensitive area.

Thankfully, the chief of police understood (he'd taken a couple of photos of the boy himself and sent them off to the National Enquirer) and simply confiscated her film.

3. Waiting for a bus, Birmingham, England

Just after midnight, sitting on my backpack outside Birmingham's grubby underground bus station waiting for the last bus to Stratford. In all my travels, this is the only time I have genuinely feared for my life.

I spent an hour or so trying not to catch the eye of the various addicts, dealers and thugs who passed by, trying to judge whether I was worth rolling or not. Finally a drunk came along and shouted me a beer at the pub just up the road—the local of all the riffraff who had just spent the past hour circling me like a pack of sharks.

214

4. Bujumbura, Burundi

We inadvertently arrived in Burundi during one of its frequent massacres. An Air France jumbo had airlifted most of the ex-pats out, the city was sealed off and all the banks and restaurants were closed. Luckily we met some Belgian aid workers who hadn't been able to get on the plane out. They took us down to the yacht club where we slept in boats and threw rocks at the hippos until things calmed down.

5. LA riots

My first trip to Los Angeles—to America in fact—coincided with the riots that consumed the city after the Rodney King trial. As I was staying in Hollywood, an area that looks like it is being constantly looted, the riots didn't really effect me—that is, until I went to the United Airways office in Beverly Hills to confirm my flight out. There, the wealthy white customers were so patronisingly nice to the only black customer—giving him their spot in the queue, saying how terrible the verdict was—that I thought he was going to hit them.

6.   Mr 'I don't you', Zaire

Bouncing about on the back of a truck in the middle of Zaire, one of my fellow passengers—an effeminate, almost pretty boy—reached over and started stroking my arm cooing 'I don't you'. I almost answered 'I don't you too' but something about the look on his face suggested that it wouldn't have been a good idea. Later in the night when he went off to the back of the truck with one of the other male passengers, I knew it wasn't.

7.   Seoul, Korea

While I was in Seoul, some students overturned cars in front of the Hilton and set them on fire. The first I heard about it was when I rang my mum back in Australia. And to think I'd come that close to checking into the Hilton—not!

8.   Fare evasion, Tokyo, Japan

This is probably the closest I've gotten to seeing the inside of a jail anywhere. Down on my cash in Tokyo—not an uncommon situation when you've only got Australian dollars—I had taken to using my rail pass for journeys it really wasn't valid for. Most ticket collectors were too polite to say anything, but not the guy at Nihombashi. He dragged me off to a small room and threatened to call the police. I called his bluff, telling him to go ahead, and ended up getting off for twice the normal fare. My only defence is that the Australian dollar had been taking one of its customary batterings at the time.

215

9.   Ephesus, Turkey

A couple of friends and I thought it would be a lark to see if we could get into the ruins of the ancient city of Ephesus on the Aegean coast of Turkey for free. We'd snuck into the open-air museum in Göreme but that had been easy. Ephesus proved to be much more of a challenge.

We tagged onto the end of a group of German tourists to get through the gate, but as I wasn't wearing loud shorts and a baseball cap, our cover was soon blown. A guard scurried after the group and asked the tour guide to identify us. To save the others, I separated myself from the group and 'confessed' that I thought it was free. After paying admission, I then spent the rest of the afternoon secretly meeting them around the ruins, including one particularly furtive meeting in the ancient toilet.

10. Hookers in Java, Indonesia

One night when I was walking back to my losmen in Java, Indonesia, I was accosted by two hookers from Madura. Since I was heading that way, I started up a conversation with them, hoping to get a few hints on the sights. Unfortunately, my understanding of Bahasa Indonesian at that stage didn't extend beyond 'Berapa harganya', which, roughly translated, means 'How much?'. Let me tell you, it's not the thing to say to two ugly hookers on a slow night in Probolinggo. I barely escaped with my life.

Chapter 22

TRAVELLING COMPANIONS

Travel can be a daunting experience when you're on your own. There's accommodation to find, buses to catch and that little matter of the sleazy local sitting on the other side of the restaurant leering at you. Better, one would think, to share all this with someone you know and love.

There is a dark side to travelling together—the moods, the fights, the compromises. Here's your guide to the tricky dilemma of travelling with someone.

Should I travel with someone?

Travelling with right person can be a wonderful thing, adding a whole new dimension to the travel experience. If you're travelling with your partner, beachside sunsets will be rosier and if you're travelling with mates, big nights out will be wilder and more debauched. Travelling with the wrong person, however, can be like getting trapped in the Big Brother house with the most annoying contestant without any hope of ever being evicted.

Is there anyone I shouldn't travel with?

In truth, there are probably more people you shouldn't travel with than you should. They include:

o **Deranged psychopaths:** Nothing ruins a trip faster than travelling with someone who snaps at the smallest provocation or harangues shopkeepers and hotel managers simply for the fun of it. Just ask the people I've travelled with.

217

- o **International drug runners:** Can make crossing borders a little difficult, especially if they ask you to carry a small parcel across for them.

- o **Born-again Christians:** Tend to put a dampener on big nights out with their insistence on asking other patrons at the bar if they know Jesus as their Lord and personal saviour.

- o **Snorers:** You won't appreciate the importance of a good night's sleep until you've been robbed of a week's worth by someone who sounds like a blocked drain every time they get a little shut-eye.

- o **Root Rats:** Do you really want to be kept up all night by your friend's amorous activities— especially when you're not getting any?

- o **Workaholics:** They'll spend the whole trip obsessing about their work and fretting that the office is falling apart without them.

And, of course, you've got to ask yourself one very important question— do you really want to travel with someone silly enough to want to travel with you?

What makes an ideal travelling companion?

An ideal travelling companion is a lot like an ideal life partner—someone with lots of money, heaps of patience and the ability to live with all your idiosyncrasies and personality disorders.

Naturally, your chances of finding someone like that are about as good as you ever winning Lotto.

Travelling with a fake husband

In many places like Pakistan, Turkey or even Queensland, a single girl travelling on her own is seen as an open invitation by the local men to treat a girl's buttocks as a ripe cantaloupe. It used to be that wearing a wedding ring was enough to deter this unwanted attention but unfortunately international sleazeballs are now awake to this trick and it has lost its efficacy.

One way around this is to travel with a male friend and introduce him as your husband. The downside, however, is trying to explain your 'husband' to the cute guy you met down the beach or explaining to your new 'husband' that the marriage does not include conjugal rights.

Should I travel with my current partner?

One school of thought has it that there is no better way to find out about your lover than hitting the road with them. How they deal with shonky moneychangers and difficult taxi drivers can give you an invaluable insight into how they may handle your finances or a traffic jam back home.

Trouble is, there's no better way for them to find out about all your annoying habits. Don't be surprised if after three days they want go their separate way. Especially if all the traveller's cheques are in their name.

Is there a danger of 'too much too fast'?

Travelling with your partner is the equivalent of putting your relationship on fast forward. A week in a Third World shithole where the beds are mouldy and the transport is torturous is the equivalent of three years in a sad, loveless marriage.

It's worse if they get a dose of Bali Belly. Do you really want to hear the love of your life doing their best cappuccino machine impersonations? Best leave those kinds of noises until the twilight years when, after 50 years of marriage, you are about to toddle off to the old people's home and you've been using incontinence protection for decades.

219

Will we scare off the locals?

When you're travelling with someone, you become a kind of unit, caught up in your own little world. Where locals feel more at ease approaching a single traveller, they will baulk at approaching a couple, especially when they are having a blazing row over who should be reading the map.

Fortunately, this is a mixed blessing. While you will undoubtedly miss out on the odd kindly offer of a free meal or bed for the night, you will also forego the more dubious honour of being followed by an annoying tout that you just can't shake.

How will I know trouble is brewing?

Personal habits that were once tolerated or even considered quaint will begin to grate on nerves. Most conversations will start with 'You know, it's really annoying when you do that' and end with 'I don't know why I even bother trying to talk to you'. Another telltale sign is when your girlfriend starts bringing back other guys to your beach-side bungalow.

Is three a crowd?

Not necessarily. When I travelled through Central America with a girlfriend for six months, we had an English guy travel with us for six weeks. If he hadn't been there as another person to chat with, spat with and make fun of, we would have probably split up by Costa Rica, instead of three months after we got back home.

Having said that, it's not an awful lot of fun *being* that third person. I spent a month travelling with an English couple in Turkey and could feel the room physically chill when they had a fight. Of course, it could have been caused by the fact that I was obviously smitten with the girl.

The benefits of time apart

It's not natural for human beings, no matter how close, to be in each other's company 24/7. You're bound to get on each other's nerves and see and say things you rather wish you hadn't. My reaction to discovering a cache of mascara in my girlfriend's pack was a perfect example of that.

It's the same when you're travelling with friends. After travelling in Africa for three months with a couple of mates, things began getting a little gnarly, so I took off on my own for a couple of days. After three days on a petrol tanker that kept breaking down, I greeted their arrival by bus in the tiny dusty village I was stuck in like the Second Coming. And, thankfully, they seemed genuinely happy to see me too. Unfortunately, I talked them into getting a ride with a petrol tanker too and all the benefit from a bit of down time was undone.

220

I can't suggest that to my partner, they'd kill me!

True, suggesting a little time apart is more difficult when it's your partner. Any hint that it might be a good idea to head off in different directions could give the idea that you're questioning the whole relationship. Still, better to have a few days apart in India than a messy divorce once you get back home involving the kids and the labrador.

Tell me about travelling with mates

It sounds ideal. Travelling with someone you know and like and have a history of having a good time with. It'll be just like back at home—you'll go out drinking and carousing, only this time in a foreign local.

But how well do you know the person? I once travelled with an old school buddy who was famous for always turning up an hour late. It got so chronic that we began to tell him that we were meeting somewhere an hour earlier than we really intended to show up. Back home it was all very quaint and funny. But when we had to catch a once-a-week bus out of a hellhole in Tanzania and he was still practising packing his bag, I no longer saw the funny side.

So how did it wash up? As far as I know, he's still there!

221

And family?

Remember the last Christmas when all the family got together? Well, travelling with a parent or a sibling is that, times one hundred. Do you really want your mum reminding you to brush your teeth in front of your cool, new traveller friends? Or spend two weeks on a beach in Thailand listening to your sister explaining to you why you can't find a partner?

Surely I can travel with someone I meet while travelling?

Probably your best bet, mainly because you're both likely to be heading in the same direction and it helps cut down the accommodation costs. And if they begin to bug you it's easy to invent a reason to split up without the acrimony that goes with suggesting some time apart from family, friends or lovers.

Trouble is, you don't really know them from Adam. You could end up going through your stuff a few weeks later and discover that your Maglite is missing.

TOP 10 TIPS FOR TRAVELLING WITH BLOKES

Blokes like to think they are easy-going and easy to travel with, but quite the opposite is true. If we are to be honest—and we're amongst friends here, so why not?—men are the orneriest, crankiest and most stubborn travelling companions you'll ever find. With that in mind, I offer the following insider tips so that if you ever find yourself in such circumstances, you can at least make it bearable.

1. Let him climb things

Put a man in front of a mountain or an ancient temple and he will feel compelled to climb it. Something in our DNA compels us to conquer things—the same thing that made your man pursue you so ardently when you were first dating. Of course, you won't see the sense in expending so much energy so unnecessarily, but don't waste your time trying to argue him out of it. Just tell him that you'll be waiting at the bottom with an ice-cold beer and a CPR unit for when he staggers back down.

2. Don't show him your packing list

Never let a list of what you are intending to take away with you fall into your partner's hands. In fact, commit it to memory and never write it down in the first place. Your man will never understand the need for a hairdryer and a decent face cleanser, let alone the absolute necessity of a second pair of espadrilles. He will then spend every waking minute of the two weeks before you go pruning your list like the treasurer with health expenditure before budget night.

222

3. Never let him pick up your bag

Even if you are allowed to take everything on your list, your bag will be lighter than his. Every time he has to lift it into the boot of a taxi or off the luggage carousel at the airport he'll complain that he has to carry all the heavy stuff and insist that you carry his laptop.

4. Let him read the maps

As with climbing things, men have an innate need to be in charge of directions. They like to think they are in control at all times. So rather than being berated with questions like 'Are you sure this is the right way?' let him do all the navigating. Not only do you avoid the stress of finding your way around a strange city, it also puts you in a position of power when he inevitably gets it wrong and you spend hours crossing and re-crossing the Brooklyn Bridge.

5. Don't gloat when he gets it wrong

This will only result in the kind of spiteful and juvenile fight you'd thought you'd left behind in the schoolyard. He'll be feeling embarrassed and ashamed enough as it is, and will go out of his way to take your mind off his mistake. Use this to your advantage to get a nicer hotel or that leather handbag you spotted down at the markets.

6. Let him do the haggling

Back home getting him to buy a new shirt is like pulling teeth, but put a bloke in a dusty, humid market in Asia where the prices are highly negotiable and he'll turn into a super-shopper. It will become a point of honour for him to get you that batik sarong for a price that will make the stall-holder weep. In fact, he'll probably enjoy it so much you'll end up with an entire new wardrobe that he'll pay for because it was 'so much fun'.

223

7. Be prepared to play nurse when he's sick

Think of what he's like when he's sick back home and multiply it by ten. He'll be convinced he has got some exotic disease when all he's got is a dose of the runs. Not only that, you'll be expected to mop his brow, buy him drinks and go to the local chemist to candidly explain his symptoms to a shop assistant who usually only sells sunblock. As with when he gets directions wrong, make sure you use it to your advantage and insist he'd be more comfortable in a room with an attached bathroom, air-conditioning and room service.

8. Don't expect sympathy when you're sick

While they are the biggest sooks on earth when they're sick, blokes are the world's worst nurses. When you come down with a dose of the Russian Flu he'll probably get annoyed that you're disrupting the day's plans. Having said that, if you get really sick, he'll move heaven and earth to get you to a hospital—even if you're out the back of Bourke and it means commandeering the Flying Doctor's Cessna to get you there.

9. Don't nick his food or drink

Nothing aggravates a bloke more than someone pilfering his food or slogging back his drink—especially when his kind offer to buy you your own has been refused. If you're worried that you wouldn't finish an entire serving on your own, don't. Your fella will help you polish that one off as well.

10. Let him sit next to the window

Men tend to be in a better mood if they can look out the window and watch the world go by. They're even happier if there's a window they can open. Must be the labrador genes.

(OK, so this is probably just my particular fetish. Probably best if you ignore this advice.)

Chapter 23

THE INTERNET

From yurts in Mongolia to mud huts on the shores of Lake Malawi in Africa, there aren't many places in the world that aren't wired up and online. Word is that even the Amish have set up an Internet cafe up in Pennsylvania and plan to open it once they finally get the power on. Here's your guide to travelling in a connected world.

Has the Internet changed travel?

It sure has. There was a time not so long ago when the first thing a traveller would do when they rolled into a new town was check out the closest bar and maybe find a room. Today's traveller however, won't really feel at home until they've found the nearest Internet cafe and checked their emails. Instead of bragging about how many countries they've visited, travellers now boast about how many emails they got that day. It's a new world out there, and if you haven't got a Hotmail account—or something similar—you're missing out.

The NSITT guide to effective Internet usage

Let me just say that I'm a big fan of the Internet. I love the fact that I was able to log in on a crappy old computer in a dusty Mayan village and find out about the birth of my latest nephew back home. In that way alone it has saved me a fortune on international calls (Australia is *always* in the most expensive zone!)

But there are heaps of other ways a canny traveller can use the Internet to make their trip more enjoyable and last longer. For example, you can use the Internet to:

o   Email your mum and dad for more money.

225

o   Taunt your workmates with tales about what a great time you're having.

o   Visit a medical site and check if that rash really is fatal.

o   Organise a piss-up with the other travellers you met a few days before.

o   Check whether your bank balance is really as dire as you think it is.

o   Line up a bed at a friend's place in London, New York or Sydney.

o   Check the weekend results of your favourite team. (Having said that, if you follow the football teams I follow then that can be a bad thing. A very bad thing.)

There must be a downside

Sure. It's a lot easier for your boss to contact you and tell you that you're needed back at the office immediately. And with marks and grades now readily available over the Internet, you can instantly know that you'll be doing first year Psych all over again.

Then there are all the little idiosyncrasies of accessing the Internet while you're away. You won't be able to find an Internet cafe when you're waiting on an important email. And they'll be everywhere when you haven't got enough money to use them. The more expensive it is to access the Internet, the crappier the connection. The connection always drops out when you're sending or receiving a large file. When you find a cheap connection you won't receive any emails and you won't have any to send.

And Hotmail is invariably, inevitably, always painfully slow.

Why *is* Hotmail so slow?

226

Most people think it's because there are so many people using the service throughout the world. But the fact is that Microsoft is simply helping Third World countries reduce debt. Word is that the good folk at Redmond deliberately slow down access times to travellers checking their emails in exotic and far flung locales. Hence, the more costly the connection, the slower the connection. It's true!

How much of my budget should I allocate for accessing the Internet?

Unfortunately, most of it—especially if you have a Hotmail account! One of the sad things about the introduction of the Internet is that travellers are now spending more money on checking their email account than getting pissed. On a recent trip to Antigua in Guatemala I was disturbed to notice that while all the Internet cafes were full—their patrons staring into monitors with their backs to the colourful colonial streetscapes outside—the bars were empty. Now that's just wrong!

227

Is my email name important?

Definitely. Chances are you'll be drunk when you're handing it out—and so too will the person you're giving it to. So obviously it should be something easy to remember and easy to spell.

Of course, your own name would be ideal, but as anyone who has recently tried to subscribe to Hotmail knows, it's almost impossible to get your name, especially if you've got a common-as-muck name like mine. I was offered petermoore_23492755472290@hotmail.com the last time I tried.

You could try for something cute or funny, but chances are that'll wear thin. A friend of mine used his girlfriend's pet name for him, but they've since broken up and mrfluffymuffy@yahoo.com just raises more questions than it answers when he hands it out to people he meets on the road.

Is there anyone I should never, ever give my email address to?

Strange as it may seem, there *are* some people you should never, ever give your email address to. Basically, they're the people you left home to get away from. And, much to the chagrin of Internet cafes the world over, I'm listing them below.

o   **Your Aunt Beatrice:** All you'll get are long drawn-out stories about your cousin's court case and Uncle Bob's upcoming operation. If she's got a scanner, you'll get pictures of the X-rays and doctor's reports as well.

o **Anyone with a newborn baby:** Your inbox will be clogged up with pictures of the sprog—its first steps, its first birthday, even its first teeth. Worse, the pictures will be huge 'cos the proud parents want to make sure you see all the details. Particularly scary with the mandatory breastfeeding shot.

o **The folk back at the office:** Sure, you'll get the latest gossip, but you'll also get all those weak jokes and humungous files that turn out to be nothing more than singing hamsters. Fine when you're trying to put off working, but a real nuisance when you're paying $1 a minute on a flaky connection that keeps dropping out.

o **Your ex:** A bitter, vengeful letter listing all your faults in graphic detail is the last thing you want on your holidays. Especially when a 'new' holiday acquaintance is sitting beside you when you check your mail.

o **Your creditors:** Best to find out after you get back that your stereo has been seized to pay off unpaid parking fines. Not much you can do about it 20,000 kilometres away, is there?

o **The drunken mistake:** You were plastered and not thinking straight. The last thing you want is an ongoing cyber affair with someone who, quite frankly, was a dud in real life. Your only hope is that in your inebriated state you garbled your email address or put all the dots in the wrong place.

What if nobody sends me emails?

Nothing is sadder than the person who rocks up to an Internet cafe, coughs up for the minimum half hour and then doesn't have any new messages in the inbox. They've got to spend the next 27 minutes reading the latest on the on-line version of their local newspaper, or catching up on the progress of *Star Wars Episode 2* on the George Lucas fan site.

228

If it really bothers you, why not use all that spare time to subscribe to heaps of newsletters? Then, next time you open your Hotmail account you can proudly exclaim 'Wow! 139 new messages!' Just make sure to hide the senders' names and subject headers from the admiring glances of nearby surfers.

What else can I do to kill time in an Internet cafe?

If you should find yourself with half an hour to kill, there are many ways to amuse yourself.

o   Click on the history button and see where your fellow travellers have been. If you're lucky, someone's online bank might have a piss-weak security and let you log back in.

o   Read somebody else's email over their shoulder. Much more annoying than reading the paper of the person next to you on the tube and more fun to boot.

o   Go to Windows Explorer and have a squiz around the C drive. You'll be amazed what you can stumble across, especially in folders entitled 'Secret Stuff'.

o   Call the proprietor over and tell them that you think you've just downloaded a virus.

o   Laugh raucously while pretending to read your emails. Not only will it disturb fellow surfers, it will make them wish that their friends were so funny.

o   Check the favourites and count how many porn sites the guy running the place has bookmarked.

Of course, you could do something constructive with your time and visit a really useful website.

What *are* the most useful websites while travelling?

Funnily enough, when you're paying the equivalent of a month's wages, your surfing habits change. While you may mindlessly trawl through porn sites and download MP3's on your computer at work, you get a little more pragmatic on the road. Personally, I rarely go beyond checking my emails and dropping by the *Sydney Morning Herald* online (Australian news never makes any international papers!). If I really have to, I check my bank account, but only if I'm sober.

Surely online banking is a boon to travellers?

It is, especially if, like me, you drag most of your money out of foreign ATMs, not altogether sure of what the rate is, or how much you have left in your account. It's just that when you're travelling on Australian dollars, it's never a pretty sight. I've found that bank balances are a bit like cholesterol levels. You really should know what they are, but knowing how dire they are can seriously curtail your fun.

Should I use the Internet to do work while I'm away?

I've got to say, the Internet has been great for me. I'm actually writing this in Cairo and will be sending it to my publishers from a scungy Internet cafe just off Midan Talaat Harb. But if you're like 99.9 per cent of the population who travel to get away from mundane things like work and study, best to tell your boss or tutor that there'll be no Internet access where you're going, and hope that they don't realise that there's no place in the world where that's true any more.

What about using the Internet to book accommodation?

In theory, it sounds great. Log into the website for a hostel or hotel in the next town you're going to and book a room. You turn up after an 18-hour bus trip, and, voila, there's a bed waiting for you.

Unfortunately, it never works like that. No one ever checks the email at the said establishment or, more usually, the computer was wiped out months before by a virus that the night manager downloaded while he was looking at porn.

230

TOP 10
INTERNET CAFES

What makes a great Internet cafe? Is it a fast connection, where your Hotmail account opens within minutes rather than hours? Is it access rates that allow you to surf the net for an hour and still afford a beer or two that night? The condition of the computers? The general ambience?

Sometimes it's all those things and at other times none of them. All I know is there are some Internet cafes that transcend being just a place for getting news from home. And here's ten of them.

231

1.   Public Library, Havana, Cuba

Only occasionally working—conspiracy theorists blame it on a vindictive Cuban exile hacker based in Miami—the appeal of this place is its setting in the old El Capitolio building. The smell of floor wax mingles with the fumes from old Chevvies being rebuilt on the pavement outside. Magic.

2.   On top of Table Mountain, Cape Town, South Africa

I don't exactly know why this place is here—can't imagine too many people would climb Table Mountain, or even catch the cable car up, just to check their emails. Still, the views across the top of the mountain are spectacular. And it does give you something to do when the 'table cloth' (a thick cloud of mist) invariably descends on the mountain.

3.   Death Metal Cafe, Bucharest, Romania

Down some rickety stairs and in a dark and dingy basement where the walls are painted black, this place is cheap and, to be brutally honest, nasty. Chances are the guy on the terminal next to you will have an extensive collection of tats and body piercings and is watching a live webcast of a Black Sabbath concert.

4. Bob's Place, Ölüdeniz, Turkey

Decked out like a Turkish harem, with wispy curtains and thickly embroidered throw cushions, this cafe is high on ambience but low on ergonomics. Still, the well-stocked bar is only metres away and the view of the aqua blue Mediterranean outside will remind you that there is more to life than downloading some pathetic joke from the folk back at the office.

5. Corporate Computer Services, Addis Ababa, Ethiopia

Despite the impressive name, this place is nothing special—old Pentium 150 computers and a connection as slow and unreliable as the local bus service—but it's still not a bad place to while away the hours during one of the frequent student riots. If you're lucky they might even overturn and torch a car right out front as you surf.

6. Cafe on Main Street, Panajachel, Guatemala

What's cool about this place is that while you're accessing Yahoo or Hotmail, the locals are wandering by in brightly embroidered clothes going about their business as they have done for centuries. Cool.

7. Gracias Internet Cafe, Barcelona, Spain

Set just off a quaint square—complete with a medieval clock tower that you can use to keep track of how long you've been surfing—this is the cheapest Internet cafe in Barcelona. Of course, like everywhere in Spain it is always filled with smoke. But if you like, the friendly owner will sell you one of the smuggled Cuban cigars he keeps under the counter so you can add to it. You've got to admit, there's something decidedly decadent about sucking on a stogey while checking your emails.

8. Blue Tiled Cafe, Stone City, Zanzibar

232

Fast, cheap and with an airconditioner set on Arctic levels, this is a great place to escape the heat of tropical Zanzibar. Doesn't seem to have a name, so just look for the place completely decked out in blue tiles run by a friendly Indian lady. Enjoy!

9.   POP2000, Luxor, Egypt

The cheapest place in town and overlooking the ruins of Luxor Temple, this place is made special by the way the owner insists on playing a CD of a guy singing Koranic verses as you surf. If you're really lucky he'll let you play his Haj CD-Rom, a multimedia and interactive tour of Mecca.

10.   My mate Keith's place, London, England

His 366 Pentium is getting a bit long in the tooth and the 28.8k modem could do with upgrading, but hey, he lets me use his connection for free. And with the Aussie dollar struggling at close to three to one with the pound, that's a very good thing.

233

234

Chapter 24

TOURS

Going on an organised tour is seen by many as an anathema to the independent travelling ideal. Designated toilet breaks just don't seem to gel with the idea of hitting the road and seeing what happens. But in the face of no time, no money or no way to get between point A and B, many independent travellers are forced to consider the dreaded tour option. Here's advice on how to do a tour and save your world traveller cred—or if you'd prefer, have a good time and get laid.

235

What is a tour?

A tour is basically travelling with all the hard bits taken out. Someone else organises your bed for the night and your meals for the day and deals with petty border officials and corrupt policemen. It doesn't always involve getting onto a crowded tour bus wearing a name tag and introducing yourself to a bunch of people wearing Born Again Christian smiles, but it can do.

Why go on a tour?

Going on a tour is not for everybody, especially for those of us who actually enjoy haggling with touts or sitting on a deserted stretch of road waiting for a bus that may never come.

Some reasons why you might consider going on a tour include:

o   Your lousy boss will only give you two weeks off and your unpaid student debts mean you can't tell him where to stick his job.

- You're a sad, antisocial creature who can't make friends easily.
- You've always had a thing for tour guides, Overland truck drivers or cooks. (Saddo!)
- The only other option for getting where you want to go involves waiting for a ride at a dusty truck stop for six weeks.
- You're quite partial to instant noodles and dry biscuits.
- You enjoy card games, especially if they involve drinking.
- When you've had too much to drink, you feel compelled to dance on bars, or strip naked and swim in lakes riddled with bilharzia.

Tell me about Overland trucking tours

Overlanders, as they are known, are converted trucks that lug travellers through the more off-the-beaten track destinations. Common in Africa and Asia, and increasingly popular in South America, they are seen as a convenient way to travel for people with a short amount of time or for those worried about security in these areas. Governmental studies have also shown that Overlanders are instrumental in keeping the local breweries in operation.

236

Why do Overland truck drivers get all the girls?

There seems to be something in the female DNA that is drawn towards guys no matter how ugly they are, who know their way around a carburettor. Just as guys are drawn towards girls who know their way around a lap dancing routine, I guess.

Will I be given a silly nickname?

Yes. You will acquire an imaginative name like 'Chalky' (because you don't wash your underwear) or 'Big Tits' (well, just because) and it will be put on a specially printed commemorative T-shirt at the end of the tour, along with the names of other mystery guests like Di Rea and Murray J Wana. You will also be expected to do things you would never dream of doing back home—like bungy jumping and white-water rafting—and dance on the bar at various drinking establishments along your itinerary.

Will I get a shag?

Very rarely will the girl/guy ration work in your favour. And as mentioned above, you will have to compete with the driver/cook/guide for the affections of that fellow tourer you've got your eye on.

Having said that, there will be times when the above-mentioned ratio will work in your favour. I met a guy in Turkey who had just got off a Contiki tour of Europe where he was the only guy on a bus-load of 25 women. Thinking all his Christmases had come at once, he spent the entire trip getting 'acquainted' with nearly every single one of them. He thought he'd done rather well, flitting from tent to tent without the slightest hint of acrimony. Unsurprisingly, he was called all manner of names in the souvenir tour book, 'fucking using bastard' being perhaps the politest.

What tours should I avoid?

Any tour company that uses the word *eco* in their company name or brochure should be given an exceedingly wide berth. The tour will invariably be run by an overly earnest tour guide wearing long socks and boots and will be patronised by Germans wearing long socks and sandals.

I made the mistake of going on an eco-tour of Kakadu National Park in the Northern Territory. It was a very well run tour and Dave, the tour guide, was very informative. But that didn't stop me spending the entire trip wishing that I was with the tour full of English backpackers who were always twenty minutes behind us, and always with a can of VB in their hands. They probably didn't know that the Alligator River was named after the HMS *Alligator*, one of the ships that surveyed the estuaries of Van Diemen Gulf in 1837, but they were having too good a time to care.

What about day tours?

Of course, not all tours involve getting into the back of a truck with 22 other smelly travellers for weeks on end. There are other tours—destination or activity specific tours—that backpackers are likely to take, brewery tours being the most common.

237

Other popular tours include the Spice Island tour in Zanzibar (although I'm convinced travellers go on this under the misconception that some other kind of 'spices' will be on offer) and safaris to various game parks throughout Africa and Asia. British backpackers in Australia have begun taking tours to where popular Aussie soaps like *Home and Away* and *Neighbours* are filmed. But why anyone would want to go to Ramsey Street now that Anne Wilkinson has left the show, I'll never know.

Just back to the brewery tour for a minute. Will I get free beer?

This is perhaps one of the greatest fallacies in world travel, right up there with the free-love ashrams in India. Backpackers the world over have turned up at breweries the world over under the mistaken belief that there will be a free-for-all at the end of the tour. Not only is that not true, but many breweries have started charging for their tours. And what do you get for it? A boring tour through stainless steel vats and, if you're lucky, one complimentary beer at the end. At the Guinness brewery in Dublin you get a half-pint in the mock Irish pub at the end of the tour, but order any more and you'll be paying mini-bar prices.

What about getting a guide?

Most guidebooks are fairly comprehensive these days and include detailed descriptions of major sites. But if you're like me, you just haven't got the attention span to follow them (I usually give up after failing to figure out exactly where I am in the said museum, monument or temple). That's when a local guide can be quite useful for pointing out stuff you may otherwise have missed.

Having said that, getting a guide isn't easy. Some places offer 'official' guides, armed with a nifty laminated badge they just got made up down the road, but they charge 'official', that is, officially over-inflated, prices. 'Unofficial' guides are cheaper but sometimes you get exactly what you pay for—and maybe a carpet you didn't intend on buying as well.

The NSITT guide to guides

In the course of my travels I have found that guides fall roughly into the following categories:

o **The knowledgeable, personable guide:** Knows what they're talking about and presents facts in an interesting and intriguing way. Knows when your attention is beginning to waver and moves on or throws in a salacious tidbit to regain your attention. Very rare.

o **The know-it-all guide:** Knows a lot and insists on letting you know it. Drones on and on about obscure details that even a PhD student on the topic would blanche at. Ignores the fact that you are shuffling uncomfortably from foot to foot or that half the group have wandered off to find a bar. Quite common.

o **The know-nothing guide:** Basically just some bloke who has figured out that if he hangs around tourist sites and bugs tourists enough they will give him money for pointing out obvious stuff like 'That is a temple' and 'That is a shrine'. Usually has a close family member in need of a major operation. Easily the most common guide.

o **The shag-happy guide:** Doesn't know much, but knows what he likes. Will spend the whole tour trying to get on to the cutest girl while ignoring everyone else's questions. Just the same, will expect a generous tip from everyone.

What about these short-break holidays?

Exceedingly popular in the UK and increasingly so in Australia, these packages offer little more than a cheap airfare and a week's worth of accommodation in some suitably sunny destination.

What they don't tell you is that your flight will leave from a regional airport that costs more to get to than the entire cost of your trip and that your 'waterfront' accommodation backs onto a smelly canal three kilometres from the beach you thought it would be overlooking.

239

TOP 10 FAVOURITE TOURS

Not being a big fan of tours (my attention span is such that I usually 'do' museums and art galleries in 15 minutes or less) there was something special about these ten particular tours that made being herded around like a sheep worthwhile.

1. Literary Pub Crawl, Dublin, Ireland

Writers the world over are partial to a tipple, but in Ireland their literary figures are big drinkers. From Joyce to McCourt, they all had their favourite pub and on this tour you get to visit them all. Goes to show that seeing where Oscar Wilde drank the occasional Pimms is as good a reason as any to have another pint of Guinness.

2. Livingston's 'Eco' tour, Bocas Del Toro, Panama

After the holier-than-thou eco-friendliness of neighbouring Costa Rica, this eco-hostile tour run by a huge black guy with perpetually red eyes called Livingston is a real treat. Fret as he lumbers after rare red tree frogs. Gasp as he pokes sleeping sloths with pointy sticks. And marvel as he knocks back bottle after bottle of Soberana at the mandatory piss-up at his mate's crappy built-over-the-water restaurant.

3. Grass Routes Township Tour, Cape Town, South Africa

Even though the days of apartheid are long past, it's still not a good idea to wander into one of South Africa's notorious townships. Outsiders, especially those with cameras around their necks, are still regarded with suspicion.

240

241

Thankfully, an enterprising woman called Vicki in Khayelitsha—the huge squatter camp on the edges of Cape Town—has come up with the idea of taking people on tours to show them township life, up close and personal. The tour visits the local markets, hospital and library, and finishes up at 'The Waterfront', the rough and ready *shebeen* (illegal bar). I ended up spending an afternoon drinking the cheapest beer in South Africa and playing pool with my new best friend—a guy who insisted his name was Elvis!

4.   House of the People, Bucharest, Romania

An obscenely over-the-top building, this 'palace for the people' built by the Ceaucescus is the second largest structure in the world after the Pentagon. Old Nicolae bankrupted his country building it and, despite yourself, you'll marvel at the 2000 square metre Alexandru Iaon Cuza Hall with its 18-metre-high gilded ceiling.

Another marvel are the gorgeous tour guides, none of whom would look out of place on an international catwalk. My guide, the lovely Marta, spent most of the tour fending off the advances of an Israeli film-maker keen to sign her up for a feature film. Apparently it was the fifth time he'd taken the tour that day.

5.   Duck Tour budget safari, Masai Mara, Kenya

Two days into this tour and the lions and elephants had become a little bit like cathedrals in Europe—seen one and you've seen them all. Luckily someone on our tour noted that a guy in one of the other vans circling this huge park bore an uncanny resemblance to the pugilist 'Aussie' Joe Bugner, albeit in his younger days. We spent the rest of the trip having contests as to who could spot 'Young Joe' first—ignoring the lions, buffalo, elephants and zebras our guide was desperately trying to draw our attention to.

I guess you had to be there.

6. Bob Marley Museum, Kingston, Jamaica

This overly reverential tour around Bob's old Kingston digs was largely unremarkable until we hit the kitchen and were told that his Bobness's second favourite colour combination was brown and beige. Apparently Philips don't make toasters in red, green, yellow and black.

7. Cohiba Factory, Havana, Cuba

Sadly, no virgins rolling cigars on their thighs, just old aged pensioners with their teeth in glasses beside them and photos of Che stuck on the front of their work-benches. But keep an eye out for the workers who will call you over and surreptitiously sell you $50 Esplindidos for a buck.

8. Erg Chebbi, Merzouga, Morocco

Erg Chebbi is Morocco's only genuine Saharan sand dune and the perfect place to live out your Lawrence of Arabia fantasies. It's a bugger getting up at 4 am to be there in time for sunrise, and the climb to the top will nearly kill you but the run back down is well worth it.

9. The Kramer Reality Tour, New York

Run by the guy called Kramer who *the* Kramer from *Seinfeld* was based on, this is a grand tour of all the places made famous by that TV show. There's the diner where Kramer and Newman bought black-market Commander 450 shower heads, and the parking lot where George discovered that his car had been used as a brothel. There's the Y, where George and Jerry first meet Keith Hernandez, and, finally, Tom's Restaurant, the cafe where the gang obsesses over the minutiae of their lives.

The tour ends with a slice of the Real Kramer's Low Fat Vegetarian Pizza. And in the grand tradition of the harebrained schemes of the TV Kramer, it can be bought frozen, back at the theatre just off Broadway where the tour begins and ends.

10. Mentawi Tribes, Siberut, Indonesia

A tiny island off the west coast of Sumatra, Siberut is noted for its thick rainforest and colourful tribespeople. Cut off from the rest of the world, they live as they have done for centuries, in wooden longhouses and in nothing more than bark loincloth.

It's a hard slog into the jungle to get there, but you've got to love a tour where you can dress up in a loincloth and hunt monkeys with bows and arrows. Animal rights folk fret not: we were in more danger from the arrows than the monkeys.

243

FIVE
FREQUENTLY
ASKED QUESTIONS

If there's one thing wrong with travelling it's that it gives you too much time to think. Stranded on a barge or trapped on a broken down bus, you can't help pondering on life's eternal questions, like 'What the hell am I doing here?' and 'Where the hell do I get off?'.

Of course, there are other questions that are as individual as your very own neuroses yet as universal as our most fundamental fears. And here's where you'll finally find the answers to the questions that keep going through your mind. Well, five of them at least.

1.   Should I keep a journal?

Confronted by strange sights and sounds, and the odd personal habits of the people they meet, many travellers are tempted to keep a written record of their feelings and observations. Some even feel compelled to read them out loud to the people around them.

All I can say is, don't do it. Just remember that most of your scribblings will be done under the influence of alcohol, lust or some very strange drugs and are never as philosophical in retrospect as they were at the time. Only keep a journal if you want to be laughed at by your children and grandchildren in years to come.

2.   I don't look like my passport photo. Is that a problem?

No. The truth is you never looked like your passport photo. And most immigration officials know it.

In fact, there may be occasions when you will be able to use this to your advantage. When I was in Afghanistan, the guy I was travelling with didn't have a photo for a visa to get back into

245

Pakistan. So I gave him one of mine. Even though he had short hair and I had long hair and I used the same photo on my application, the Pakistani Consul didn't even question it.

3. What if I get bored?

Unbelievable as it may seem, there will come a time in your travels when the thought of looking at another temple, cathedral or colourfully dressed local will bore you rigid. Thankfully, it doesn't take much to invent a mindless game that will keep you amused for minutes and re-enthuse you once again for the whole travelling process.

246

One of my favourites is 'Spot the Celebrity'. This is a game that can be played alone or in a group and involves spotting travellers who bear a resemblance—uncanny or otherwise—to a famous person. On a tiresome boat journey off Nha Trang in Vietnam I spotted a Frenchman who looked like Arnold Schwarzenegger, a bloke reminiscent of Phil Collins and, most incredible of all, a female Bill Murray.

4. Should I give my real addresss to people I meet?

As you wander around the globe you will meet many people who will ask you for your address. Some will be fellow travellers, keen to line up a free bed when they pass through your home town. Others will be local people with an eye to nominating you as a sponsor when they try to immigrate to your country. Many are simply after footwear. A friend of mine is still receiving letters from an Indonesian family he met five years ago begging him for shoes.

So what you've got to remember when you are confronted with this dilemma is that people will not ask you for your address unless they want something. The only time I would recommend doing it is when that something is you—and the feeling is reciprocal.

5. How can I cure homesickness?

There will be times when you are on the road—usually just after a particularly humiliating cavity search—when you will feel like just chucking it all in and going home. You start to miss loved ones, you hanker after a favourite meal and, in very rare cases, you may even feel an unnatural compulsion to work or study.

Before you go racking up the airfare home on your credit card, just stop to consider for a moment that what you are missing is just an idealised vision of what you have back home.

If you're hanging out for a Big Mac, go to McDonald's. There's one in every corner of the globe and their meals are universally the same. If you're missing your family, just think of all the crappy Christmas presents they always give you. If you're pining for your partner, spend a few moments dwelling on their annoying habit of leaving the cap off the toothpaste. If you're getting all misty-eyed about work, think of the miserable pay cheque you used to get each fortnight.

And if all that doesn't work, just go home.

247

248

GLOSSARY

APEC

A trading bloc consisting of countries in Asia and the Pacific Rim. Promoted heavily by peripheral countries like Australia and the United States who feel they are missing out on all the action in Asia.

Ashrams

Originally places of religious retreat for Hindus, ashrams have become increasingly popular with Westerners looking to escape stress, pressure and monogamy.

ATMs

Automatic Teller Machines. Easy to find, except in parts of the Amazon basin and on Saturday nights when you need money for the cab fare home.

Ayatollah

The religious leader of the Shi'ite sect of Islam, the official religion in Iran. The most famous Ayatollah, Khomeini, is credited with bringing long beards and bushy eyebrows back to the catwalks of Teheran.

Bemo

Indonesian for small Japanese mini-van that has just failed rego for the third time.

Big Box, Little Box

A rave dance style that involves the dancer making the shape of a small box and then a large box with the hands. Not to be confused with 'The

Bricklayer' where the dancer mimics a tradesman putting up a small retaining wall.

Bilharzia

Not the name of a South African farmer, but rather a microscopic worm that burrows in through your skin, travels into your bloodstream and takes up residence in your intestine or bladder. Hangs out in rivers and dams waiting for hapless backpackers to go swimming.

Birkenstock

A particularly daggy brand of sandals favoured by Europeans. Often worn with shorts and socks.

Bucket shops

Travel agents that lure travellers with promises of cheap air tickets. If you're lucky, they'll still be there when you go to pick up your ticket.

CAAC

The Civil Aviation Administration of China is the official flag carrier of the People's Republic of China. Because of its less than perfect record, some wags have suggested that CAAC stands for China Air Always Cancels or, more disturbingly, China Air Always Crashes.

Cappadocians

Funnily enough, the people who live in Cappadocia in central Turkey.

Cay

Turkish for tea. Usually served in small tulip-shaped glasses by friendly locals at 50 metre intervals.

Chador

A black, one-piece cloak worn by Iranian woman to cover all parts of the body except the hands, feet and eyes. Though specifically designed to give no hint of body shape, some Iranian woman have taken to letting them flap open to reveal the latest Western fashions.

Cubic zirconia

250

A synthetic substitute for diamonds in jewellery. Particularly popular on home shopping networks and in the 'Wait, there's more!' style of advertising.

Cube

A quaint African phrase meaning 'cramped, airless room that may have a bed but definitely won't have a window'.

Dengue fever

Transmitted by mosquito bites, this disease starts as a fever before turning into a rash that takes over your whole body.

Dhows

Quaint wooden boats rigged with lateen sails that have changed little since medieval times. Often captained by oversexed middle-aged men with similarly medieval attitudes towards women.

Dysentery

This is diarrhoea gone ballistic. Same symptoms, but with the added bonus of blood or mucus in your stools. If you get it, go and see a doctor. It won't go away on its own.

Encephalitis

See *Japanese encephalitis*.

Fatwa

An authoritative ruling given on Islamic law by a mufti or Islamic leader. Should be avoided as it tends to cramp one's style quite considerably.

251

Feluccas

See *Dhows*.

Flying Goose

A Chinese company that makes everything from rifles and hammers through to batteries and mattresses. Look for it when quality is of no concern but cost is.

Giardia

An intestinal infection with symptoms that include a bloated stomach, watery, foul-smelling diarrhoea and frequent farting. Usually strikes just as you are making your move on a fellow traveller.

Gonorrhoea

A sexually transmitted disease that you'll have fun explaining to your partner back home.

Guru

Usually a spiritual teacher or revered mentor, although in travelling circles, it can be bestowed upon someone able to drink large amounts of alcohol.

Hard sleeper

As the name suggests, a bunk on a train that is hard to sleep on. In reality, little more than a glorified luggage rack.

Hepatitis

Currently available in A, B, C, D, E, F and G strains and expanding all the time, this viral infection that attacks your liver is quietly working on taking over the entire alphabet. It's also expanding on the ways it enters your system. At the moment it is transmitted by contaminated food or drink, or through blood and bodily fluids.

252

Homies and Ho's

Afro-American street slang for friends and their women folk. If you are an undercover narcotics officer, avoid using these terms as they are probably already passé and could see you getting caught out.

Japanese encephalitis

A mossie bites a pig then the mossie bites you. Next thing you know you've come down with this viral disease that makes you vomit and go delirious. And to think some people waste their money on drugs for the same effects.

Jihadic fighters

Fighters motivated by the desire to defend Islam or the cause of God. Not to be mistaken for those guys who have a few too many down the pub on Saturday night.

Koran

The holy book of Islam, based on revelations made to the prophet Mohammed. And that's all you'll get me to say on the matter.

Kretek

The most popular brand of clove cigarettes in Indonesia. Smoked by 99.9 per cent of the population on buses and in cinemas, as well as anywhere else the air-conditioning has broken down and fresh air is at a premium.

Lama

The name given to a spiritual leader in Tibetan Buddhism. Not to be confused with those funny woolly things in South America with long necks.

Losmen

Small family run hotels in Indonesia. In Bali they are usually in a native-style house.

Lothario

Unemployed layabouts with an inflated idea of their own attractiveness and nothing better to do than try to bed female travellers.

Matatu

Vans that patrol the streets of Nairobi masquerading as public transport. Note that two thirds of the space inside will be given over to ridiculously large speakers playing Bob Marley at unbearable levels.

Matoke

Mashed plantain bananas and maize. Second only to ugali as the most unpalatable meal on the planet.

253

Mujaheddin

Guerilla fighters in Islamic countries dedicated to supporting fundamentalism. Particularly thick on the ground in Afghanistan.

Maccas

Affectionate Australian abbreviation for the most ubiquitous fast food joint on the planet.

PanAm

One of the first international airlines ever, Pan American Airlines finally succumbed to years of crushing financial pressures in 1991. Recently back in name but not in spirit.

Pelni

The much-loved national shipping company of Indonesia. Travellers lucky enough to get hold of a Pelni timetable cherish it as the best fiction they have read in their travels.

Pivnice

A Czech pub.

PKK

The rebel group fighting for a separate Kurdish homeland. Responsible for the heavy military presence in Eastern Turkey and the tacky sentimental postcards the soldiers send home to their wives and girlfriends.

Plimsoll Line

A line on the side of a ship showing the legal limit of submersion. Rarely seen in lesser-developed countries and often roundly ignored when it exists.

Raki

An aniseed-flavoured grape brandy drunk copiously in Turkey. Similar to Greek ouzo, it is cheap, nasty and hell the next morning.

Refugio

A hostel, hut or shelter for mountaineers in South America.

Sadhu

A wandering Hindu holy man, sage or ascetic.

Sake

A Japanese alcoholic drink made from rice.

Secret Rapture, The

According to some of the more radical Pentecostals, there won't be a Second Coming. God will just spirit away the true believers and take them straight to heaven—even if they happen to be flying a plane or driving a car at the time.

Shifta

Somali bandits who pretty much do as they please.

Swami

A Hindu saint or religious teacher.

Siyad Barre

Leader of Somalia from 1969 to 1991 and the last guy able to impose some sort of 'order' on the place.

Slacks

Totally uncool trousers that most guidebooks assume you have a wardrobe full of.

Steins

Oversized earthenware mugs especially for beer.

Syphilis

Another sexually transmitted disease you'll have fun explaining to your partner.

Teutonic

Typically German—that is, mechanical, emotionless and infuriatingly efficient.

Tsetse fly

An African fly that feeds on human blood and whose bite can induce sleeping sickness.

Two-pot screamer

Someone unable to handle even the smallest amounts of alcohol. Look it up in the dictionary and chances are you'll see my name mentioned.

255

Tuk-tuk

Three-wheeled bug-shaped vehicles that contribute generously to the levels of noise and air pollution in Bangkok.

Ugali

A tasteless mixture of maize and water that leaves you feeling leaden and queasy. Unfortunately, it will be your staple diet in Africa.

Yobbo

Loud, obnoxious, loutish. An Australian male by any other name.

Wallahs

People in India charged with doing a specific task or business. A dhobi-wallah, for example, is responsible for taking your laundry and beating it to within an inch of its life.

256

ANYTHING
TO DECLARE?

(Visit NSITT on the Web)

If you've got access to the Internet, **NSITT** gives you the opportunity to get all interactive and share your experiences with millions of other travellers from all over the world.

Just point your browser to **http://www.noshit.com.au** and you're in the wonderfully perverse world of **NSITT** on the web.

If you want to share a travelling experience, go to **Group Therapy.** There you'll have the opportunity to comment on each of the topics in this book or add a suggestion to one of the top tens.

If you think I've got it wrong, visit **Anything to Declare?** and vent your spleen. Similarly, if you want to say something nice, you can do that too.

The **NSITT** web site is also a fun place to visit. There are heaps of links to useful travel information as well as weird postcards, strange packages and travellers with appalling dress sense. In fact, it's a lot like a trip to Bali.

So come on, visit **NSITT** on the Internet and share your travelling experiences with the world. You never know, it could be therapeutic. But chances are, it will just be a laugh for the rest of us.

See you in cyberspace.

THE WRONG WAY HOME
by Peter Moore

When Peter Moore announced he was going to travel home from London to Sydney without stepping on to an aeroplane he was met with a resounding Why? The answer was a severe case of hippie envy: hippies had the best music, the best drugs, the best sex. But most of all, they had the best trips.

Knowing that his funds were woefully inadequate and that his chances of actually making it through such notorious hot-spots as the Balkans, Iran and Afghanistan were, in a word, slim, Peter was never one to err on the side of caution and over the next eight months (and twenty-five countries) he followed the trail overland to the East. It would prove to be a journey of exhilarating highs and, on occasions, frustrating lows, of diverse experiences – including the world's most expensive disco (in Albania), the bombed-out villages of Croatia, the opium fields of Laos, student riots in Jakarta, an all-night beach rave on a small island in Thailand – and memorable encounters with a wonderful cast of often eccentric, at times exasperating and, once in a while, overly amorous characters.

Funny, irreverent and acutely observed, *The Wrong Way Home* will strike a chord with anyone who has ventured on such a life-enhancing Grand Tour. It will also entertain (and perhaps alarm) all those who love to read about such adventures but would never be fool enough to grab that rucksack and go.

A Bantam paperback
0553 81238 6

THE FULL MONTEZUMA
by Peter Moore

'Moore's a sharp observer of the bizarre . . . read, enjoy, escape'
Maxim

Intrepid travel writer Peter Moore recently invited the new love of his life, a.k.a. the girl next door, to join him on a romantic sojourn through Central America. The trip would take them into an area of the world emerging from decades of civil war, an area racked with poverty, disease and natural disasters. Naturally, she jumped at the chance.

Over the next six months they battled hurricanes, mosquitoes, uncooperative border officials and over-sexed Mexican commuters, and along the way they learnt rather more about each other than they really wanted to . . . From Zapatista rebel heartlands in Mexico to a quiet game of cricket in Jamaica, from the devastation wrought by Hurricane Mitch in Honduras to breathtaking ancient Mayan sites and perfect golden Caribbean beaches, *The Full Montezuma* chronicles the highs and lows of one couple's journey into the unknown. Written with Moore's wicked sense of humour and his eye for the bizarre, and punctuated by a roll call of annoying habits – map-hogging, over packing, bite-scratching and over-zealous haggling – *The Full Montezuma* is hilarious, incisive and acutely observed, a cautionary tale for anyone planning to cross a continent with their significant other.

A Bantam paperback
0553 81335 8

LET THERE BE LITE
by Rupert Morgan

'Rupert Morgan's satire of modern life is brilliant. He is like Ben Elton at his wittiest but minus the worthiness: although he makes salient points about our time, taking swipes at democracy, big business, justice and celebrity – you don't feel as if they are being rammed down your throat. His writing is fast and his characterization superb . . . Definitely one to watch'
Express

What kind of person gets elected President of the world's most powerful nation? And, more to the point, what's he had to do to get there? What makes a software squillionaire tick? After all, once you're so rich you can do any damn thing you want, then what, exactly, do you do?

How does a burnt-out hack scraping the sordid bottom of gutter journalism's barrel live with himself? And, while we're about it, are there any heroic bank managers? What would a restaurant run by Hell's Angels be like? Can you really buy someone else's nose? And what would the Old Testament say if you were to reduce it to just one sentence?

Questions, questions. Isn't life just full of them? For the answers, you need look no further than this, Ruper Morgan's laceratingly funny first novel (and by the way, why is there a rather saucy-looking chicken on the cover?) . . .

'At its best when taking pot-shots at a wide variety of modern ills – fast food, tabloid media, downsizing, soap-opera politics . . . One of Morgan's nicer inventions is a computer program that boils down complex texts to their essentials. Its treatment of the Old Testament renders it down to: "Because I say so, that's why" '
Independent

A Bantam paperback
0 553 81284 X

KITE STRINGS OF THE SOUTHERN CROSS
by Laurie Gough

'A sensual, harrowing, inspirational trip'
Peter Moore, author of *The Wrong Way Home*

Drinking the hallucinogen kava around a campfire, sleeping in a California redwood or rolled up in a rug, hitchhiking with an Austrian goatherd, fighting off a cab driver in Kuala Lumpur, living in a Hare Krishna temple, taking an illicit dip in Sylvester Stallone's pool . . .

From a remote beach in the South Pacific, Laurie Gough recalls her award-winning journey across the globe.

On the Fijian island of Taveuni, she falls in love, but discovers that even paradise has a darker side. In the Moroccan walled city of Fez, she takes a trip on a magic carpet of a different kind, on the back of a fanatical souvenir hunter's motorbike she races across America and in Malaysia she is pursued by the devil himself.

Lauded by Time magazine as one of the new generations of intrepid young female travel writers, Laurie never shrinks from the lessons of the open road, but embraces them with humour and a wisdom beyond her years. Funny, insightful and inspiring, *Kite Strings of the Southern Cross* will appeal to free spirits and armchair travellers alike – and to anyone who has ever dreamt of trying to find heaven on earth.

'Gough is an enchanting guide, moving us rather effortlessly from one exotic site to another . . . Passionate and poetic'
San Francisco Examiner

A Bantam paperback
0553 81424 9

A SELECTED LIST OF TRAVEL WRITING
AVAILABLE FROM TRANSWORLD

99600	9	NOTES FROM A SMALL ISLAND	Bill Bryson	£7.99
99786	2	NOTES FROM A BIG COUNTRY	Bill Bryson	£7.99
99702	1	A WALK IN THE WOODS	Bill Bryson	£7.99
99808	7	THE LOST CONTINENT	Bill Bryson	£7.99
99805	2	MADE IN AMERICA	Bill Bryson	£7.99
99806	0	NEITHER HERE NOR THERE	Bill Bryson	£7.99
99703	X	DOWN UNDER	Bill Bryson	£7.99
99858	3	PERFUME FROM PROVENCE	Lady Fortescue	£7.99
81424	9	KITE STRINGS OF THE SOUTHERN CROSS	Laurie Gough	£6.99
14681	1	CASTAWAY	Lucy Irvine	£6.99
14680	3	FARAWAY	Lucy Irvine	£7.99
14595	5	BETWEEN EXTREMES	Brian Keenan & John McCarthy	£7.99
99841	9	NOTES FROM AN ITALIAN GARDEN	John Marble	£7.99
50667	6	UNDER THE TUSCAN SUN	Frances Mayes	£6.99
81250	5	BELLA TUSCANY	Frances Mayes	£6.99
81335	8	THE FULL MONTEZUMA	Peter Moore	£6.99
81238	6	THE WRONG WAY HOME	Peter Moore	£7.99
99852	4	THE ELUSIVE TRUFFLE: Travels in Search of the Legendary Food of France	Mirabel Osler	£6.99